Unions and Labor Laws

Unions and Labor Laws

Martha Bridegam, J.D.

SERIES EDITOR
Alan Marzilli, M.A., J.D.

CHELSEA HOUSE
PUBLISHERS

An imprint of Infobase Publishing

Chelsea House
An imprint of Infobase Publishing
132 West 31st Street
New York, NY 10001

Library of Congress Cataloging-in-Publication Data

Bridegam, Martha Ann.
Unions and labor laws / by Martha Bridegam.
p. cm. — (Point/counterpoint)
Includes bibliographical references and index.
ISBN 978-1-60413-511-4 (hardcover)
1. Labor unions—United States—History—Juvenile literature. 2. Labor unions—Law and legislation—United States—Juvenile literature. I. Title. II. Series.

 HD6508.25.B75 2009
 331.880973—dc22

                                2009015013

Alan Marzilli, M.A., J.D.
Birmingham, Alabama

The POINT/COUNTERPOINT series offers the reader a greater understanding of some of the most controversial issues in contemporary
American society—issues such as capital punishment, immigration,
gay rights, and gun control. We have looked for the most contemporary issues and have included topics—such as the controversies
surrounding "blogging"—that we could not have imagined when the
series began.

In each volume, the author has selected an issue of particular
importance and set out some of the key arguments on both sides of the
issue. Why study both sides of the debate? Maybe you have yet to make
up your mind on an issue, and the arguments presented in the book
will help you to form an opinion. More likely, however, you will already
have an opinion on many of the issues covered by the series. There is
always the chance that you will change your opinion after reading the
arguments for the other side. But even if you are firmly committed to
an issue—for example, school prayer or animal rights—reading both
sides of the argument will help you to become a more effective advocate for your cause. By gaining an understanding of opposing arguments, you can develop answers to those arguments.

Perhaps more importantly, listening to the other side sometimes
helps you see your opponent's arguments in a more human way. For
example, Sister Helen Prejean, one of the nation's most visible opponents of capital punishment, has been deeply affected by her interac-
tions with the families of murder victims. By seeing the families' grief
and pain, she understands much better why people support the death
penalty, and she is able to carry out her advocacy with a greater sensi-
tivity to the needs and beliefs of death penalty supporters.

The books in the series include numerous features that help the
reader to gain a greater understanding of the issues. Real-life examples
illustrate the human side of the issues. Each chapter also includes
excerpts from relevant laws, court cases, and other material, which
provide a better foundation for understanding the arguments. The

volumes contain citations to relevant sources of law and information, and an appendix guides the reader through the basics of legal research, both on the Internet and in the library. Today, through free Web sites, it is easy to access legal documents, and these books might give you ideas for your own research.

Studying the issues covered by the POINT/COUNTERPOINT series is more than an academic activity. The issues described in the books affect all of us as citizens. They are the issues that today's leaders debate and tomorrow's leaders will decide. While all of the issues covered in the POINT/COUNTERPOINT series are controversial today, and will remain so for the foreseeable future, it is entirely possible that the reader might one day play a central role in resolving the debate. Today it might seem that some debates—such as capital punishment and abortion—will never be resolved.

However, our nation's history is full of debates that seemed as though they never would be resolved, and many of the issues are now well settled—at least on the surface. In the nineteenth century, abolitionists met with widespread resistance to their efforts to end slavery. Ultimately, the controversy threatened the union, leading to the Civil War between the northern and southern states. Today, while a public debate over the merits of slavery would be unthinkable, racism persists in many aspects of society.

Similarly, today nobody questions women's right to vote. Yet at the beginning of the twentieth century, suffragists fought public battles for women's voting rights, and it was not until the passage of the Nineteenth Amendment in 1920 that the legal right of women to vote was established nationwide.

What makes an issue controversial? Often, controversies arise when most people agree that there is a problem but disagree about the best way to solve it. There is little argument that poverty is a major problem in the United States, especially in inner cities and rural areas. Yet, people disagree vehemently about the best way to address the problem. To some, the answer is social programs, such as welfare, food stamps, and public housing. However, many argue that such subsidies encourage dependence on government benefits while unfairly penalizing those who work and pay taxes, and that the real solution is to require people to support themselves.

American society is in a constant state of change, and sometimes modern practices clash with what many consider to be "traditional values," which are often rooted in conservative political views or religious beliefs. Many blame high crime rates, and problems such as poverty, illiteracy, and drug use on the breakdown of the traditional family structure of a married mother and father raising their children. Since the "sexual revolution" of the 1960s and 1970s, sparked in part by the widespread availability of the birth control pill, marriage rates have declined, and the number of children born outside of marriage has increased. The sexual revolution led to controversies over birth control, sex education, and other issues, most prominently abortion. Similarly, the gay rights movement has been challenged as a threat to traditional values. While many gay men and lesbians want to have the same right to marry and raise families as heterosexuals, many politicians and others have challenged gay marriage and adoption as a threat to American society.

Sometimes, new technology raises issues that we have never faced before, and society disagrees about the best solution. Are people free to swap music online, or does this violate the copyright laws that protect songwriters and musicians' ownership of the music that they create? Should scientists use "genetic engineering" to create new crops that are resistant to disease and pests and produce more food, or is it too risky to use a laboratory to create plants that nature never intended? Modern medicine has continued to increase the average lifespan—which is now 77 years, up from under 50 years at the beginning of the twentieth century—but many people are now choosing to die in comfort rather than living with painful ailments in their later years. For doctors, this presents an ethical dilemma: should they allow their patients to die? Should they assist patients in ending their own lives painlessly?

Perhaps the most controversial issues are those that implicate a Constitutional right. The Bill of Rights—the first 10 Amendments to the U.S. Constitution—spells out some of the most fundamental rights that distinguish our democracy from other nations with fewer freedoms. However, the sparsely worded document is open to interpretation, with each side saying that the Constitution is on their side. The Bill of Rights was meant to protect individual liberties; however, the needs of some individuals clash with society's needs. Thus, the Constitution often serves as a battleground between individuals and government officials seeking to protect society in some way. The First Amendment's guarantee of "freedom of speech" leads to some very difficult questions. Some forms of expression—such as burning an American flag—lead to public outrage, but are protected by the First Amendment. Other types of expression that most people find objectionable—such as child pornography—are not protected by the Constitution. The question is not only where to draw the line, but whether drawing lines around constitutional rights threatens our liberty.

The Bill of Rights raises many other questions about individual rights and societal "good." Is a prayer before a high school football game an "establishment of religion" prohibited by the First Amendment? Does the Second Amendment's promise of "the right to bear arms" include concealed handguns? Does stopping and frisking someone standing on a known drug corner constitute "unreasonable search and seizure" in violation of the Fourth Amendment? Although the U.S. Supreme Court has the ultimate authority in interpreting the U.S. Constitution, its answers do not always satisfy the public. When a group of nine people—sometimes by a five-to-four vote—makes a decision that affects hundreds of millions of others, public outcry can be expected. For example, the Supreme Court's 1973 ruling in *Roe v. Wade* that abortion is protected by the Constitution did little to quell the debate over abortion.

Whatever the root of the controversy, the books in the POINT/COUNTERPOINT series seek to explain to the reader the origins of the debate, the current state of the law, and the arguments on either side of the debate. Our hope in creating this series is that readers will be better informed about the issues facing not only our politicians, but all of our nation's citizens, and become more actively involved in resolving these debates, as voters, concerned citizens, journalists, or maybe even elected officials.

This volume examines laws that affect the conditions of working Americans—particularly those who belong to labor unions. Periodically, news stories highlight the dangerous and oppressive working conditions of factory workers, many of them children, in Asian countries. Conditions like these were commonplace in the United States as its industries expanded in the nineteenth century. Since that time, American workers have fought for and won the right to form unions—groups of workers who can collectively negotiate with employers for better pay, more reasonable schedules, and safer working conditions. While these laws help people who are actually working, some critics argue that the reason the United States has lost so many jobs overseas is that labor laws unfairly restrict employers. This volume explores the controversies, presenting both pro-employer and pro-worker viewpoints, moving from the roots of the labor movement to the controversy surrounding a proposed law that would eliminate employers' ability to demand a secret ballot for the creation of a union (rather than allowing the union simply to collect worker signatures).

An Overview of Unions and Labor Laws

In the early 1990s, when the industrial Midwest was losing jobs tragically fast, labor lawyer Tom Geoghegan wrote about an even worse time in American history: the Great Depression of the 1930s, a time he knew only from books and older people's stories. Back then, he wrote, the American people finally lost patience with the big companies that had driven the economy into the ground. Their representatives in Washington, D.C. finally told the companies they had to let workers organize labor unions—independent organizations of employees that would work to improve pay and working conditions. People in power accepted that Americans' rights as citizens included rights inside the workplace. But it happened because of terrible times when thousands went homeless and hungry. Geoghegan didn't want the hard times back, but he did seem sorry he had missed the excitement.[1]

In late 2007, when another economic crisis faced the nation, people again made comparisons to the Great Depression. Solid-looking investment companies have turned out to be built on deceptive economic practices. Large corporations that have often asked the government to let them alone, now want public "bail-out" money to keep their businesses afloat. In hard-hit manufacturing businesses like the auto industry, owners are pushing unions to give up money and power in exchange for fewer layoffs. Voters have elected labor-friendly candidates, including President Barack Obama.

Depression-flavored labor stories have begun to make news. For example, in December 2008 the Republic Windows and Doors factory in Chicago closed on just three days' notice. The employees claimed the company had violated their federal right to receive 60 days' warning and refused to go home. They occupied the factory for six days. This wasn't an ordinary strike, in which people refuse to go to work until a demand is met. This was an illegal sit-in that violated the owner's property rights. In a different economic climate, these former employees might just have been arrested. Instead, they got a $1.75 million settlement that brought about $7,000 to everyone at the factory who had lost a job.[2] Then a new owner announced it would reopen the factory and rehire all the former employees at the same pay rates.[3] Old labor radicals heard echoes in the Republic news of another famous strike: the huge Flint sit-down strike of 1936–37, which began the rise to power of the United Automobile Workers (UAW).[4]

("UAW" stands for a union whose name has changed. It began as the United Automobile Workers but is now formally the International Union, United Automobile, Aerospace and Agricultural Implement Workers of America, which may be found at http://www.uaw.org. In union language, an "international union" is typically the parent organization of many U.S. "locals," with non-U.S. members as well, usually in Canada and possibly Mexico.)

Union membership as a percentage of the working population in the United States peaked long ago, in 1954, at 25.4 percent of all workers and 34.7 percent of nonagricultural workers. It declined steadily from then until just recently. In 2007, union membership finally rose, just slightly, to 12.1 percent. It reached 12.4 percent in 2008. That may not sound like much but it means 739,000 more union members than in 2006.[5]

Changes in Washington might also help unions in the coming years. The Congress that took office in 2009, with a majority of Democratic members, was considering legislation that might strengthen unions. The Obama administration's secretary of labor, Hilda Solis, is a longtime labor advocate.[6] By contrast, her predecessor, Elaine Chao, was a former banker, nonprofit administrator, and government official; Chao's husband, Senator Mitch McConnell, a Republican from Kentucky, had close associations with Kentucky coal mining employers.[7]

The news from the capital had business owners wondering if they might face a combined problem: not just fewer customers in hard times, but pro-employee laws raising labor costs. Union leaders, meanwhile, had to wonder how far legal advantages could help them in an economy where high demands could force employers out of business.

And Tom Geoghegan, who wrote in the early 1990s about the Great Depression? In 2009, he ran unsuccessfully for Congress.[8]

The Outlaw Days of Labor

In order to better explain the current labor environment, it is necessary to provide a brief history of labor in the United States until 1935, when the National Labor Relations Act established the right of unions to organize and engage in "collective bargaining" with an employer on behalf of their members. It is history students should know, because labor debates are full of claims that the bad old days are back, one way or another.

The history of labor in the United States predates the founding of the nation itself. It begins with the European

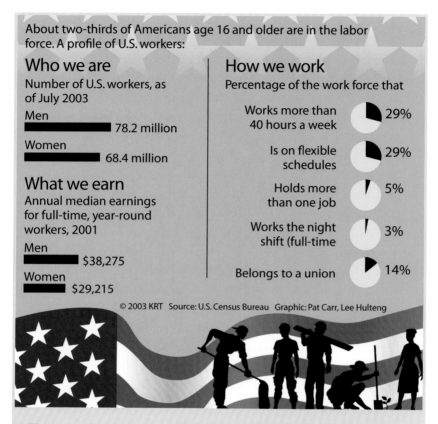

About two-thirds of Americans age 16 and older are in the labor force. A profile of U.S. workers:

Who we are

Number of U.S. workers, as of July 2003

Men
78.2 million

Women
68.4 million

What we earn

Annual median earnings for full-time, year-round workers, 2001

Men
$38,275

Women
$29,215

How we work

Percentage of the work force that

Works more than 40 hours a week — 29%

Is on flexible schedules — 29%

Holds more than one job — 5%

Works the night shift (full-time — 3%

Belongs to a union — 14%

© 2003 KRT   Source: U.S. Census Bureau   Graphic: Pat Carr, Lee Hulteng

The above graphics provide a breakdown of the American workforce, as of July 2003. Union membership has been in decline for decades but has shown a slight up-tick in recent years.

colonization of the Americas starting in the 1500s. Before the sixteenth century, money had been used more in trade than to pay directly for work. Following the colonization of the Americas, many North American workers were unpaid, whether because they were slaves or indentured servants, or because they worked in households or on farms. In fact, the first U.S. "labor organizing" consists of slaves' and indentured workers' escapes and revolts.[9]

In March 1770, British soldiers stationed in Boston, Massachusetts, shot five civilians who were protesting British interference in the colonies, including the practice of off-duty soldiers' competing for jobs with local laborers. This action would come to be known as the Boston Massacre and helped spark the American Revolution (1775–1783) against the British crown. A few years later, in 1776, Adam Smith published his classic text praising free market capitalism, *An Inquiry into the Nature and Causes of the Wealth of Nations,*[10] the same year the Founding Fathers of the United States declared independence from Great Britain and made the then-bold assertion that ordinary people, without title or wealth, could run a country.

In 1786, a few years after the peace treaty between Great Britain and the newly established United States was signed, printers in Philadelphia, Pennsylvania demanded—and received— wages of six dollars per week. Although this organized protest provided a small boost to organized labor's cause, the first U.S. labor case, the "Philadelphia Cordwainers' Case," would not occur until 1806. In it, shoemakers were fined for trying to threaten other workers into joining them in a wage demand.[11]

As the nineteenth century progressed, movements to establish better wages and working conditions developed across the United States and beyond. In the 1820s and 1830s, the standard workday for paid manufacturing workers was 12 to 14 hours. At this time the first campaigns for a 10-hour workday began.[12] Then in 1834, the first national U.S. labor organization, the National Trades Union, was founded. Changes were occurring abroad as well. With the 1848 publication of *The Communist Manifesto* by Karl Marx and Friedrich Engels in Europe, capitalism faced an economic mechanism that was its opposite, one based on common ownership and control over the means of production.[13] Contrary to Adam Smith, Marx and Engels argued that capitalism could not be made to operate fairly through social legislation, and must be abolished entirely. Around the same time, the U.S. labor movement began its split between ideological organizing and apolitical union campaigns for practical goals like wage hikes.

The most significant change in American labor occurred on January 1, 1863, when President Abraham Lincoln's Emancipation Proclamation ended legal slavery in the states that were then in rebellion against the U.S. government.[14] Two years later, in 1865, the Thirteenth Amendment to the Constitution banned "involuntary servitude" (slavery), except as a punishment for a crime, across the United States.[15] The labor movement began to pick up steam in the years after the Civil War (1861–1865), starting in 1869 with the founding of the Knights of Labor, the leading U.S. labor organization until the 1890s.

In 1875, gangster-style conflict between Pennsylvania coal miners and their employers ended with the arrests and hangings of the leaders of an Irish-American secret society, the

The Haymarket Square Riot

On May 1, 1886, activists in the Chicago labor movement held a protest in favor of the eight-hour workday. Someone in the crowd threw a bomb, which killed seven policemen. The crime, although never solved, set off a manhunt and political backlash against labor movement radicals, particularly those anarchists who had advocated political violence. Eight men were tried, and seven convicted, as accessories to murder, essentially for organizing the protest, and four were executed. People associated with unions, notably immigrants, were suspected of terrorism. Many, fearing persecution, were reluctant to join even politically moderate unions. Following the bombing, Samuel Gompers, cofounder of the relatively conservative American Federation of Labor, said, "A single bomb . . . had demolished the eight-hour movement." Years later, Governor John Peter Altgeld of Illinois pardoned some of the Haymarket prisoners. He was accused of supporting terrorists and was not reelected.

Sources: James R. Green, *Death in the Haymarket*, New York: Anchor Books, 2007; Bruce Laurie, *Artisans Into Workers*, New York: Noonday Press, 1989, pp. 168–176, 186–187 (Gompers comment, p. 170); J. Anthony Lukas, *Big Trouble*, New York: Simon & Schuster, 1997, pp. 308–309.

Mollie Maguires. The crackdown intimidated even law-abiding unions. (The story of the Mollies' infiltration by a detective from the Pinkerton Agency, a famous private investigative firm, was later fictionalized in Arthur Conan Doyle's final Sherlock Holmes novel, *The Valley of Fear*.[16]) Two years later, in July 1877, another labor dispute, the "Great Railroad Uprising," spread from West Virginia to as far as Chicago, Omaha, and the Texas city of Galveston. During the dispute, white labor groups in San Francisco attacked the homes and businesses of Chinese people, whom they viewed as low-wage competitors; in St. Louis, a general strike (a strike including many, even most, industries, and workplaces in a given area) began with the socialist Workingmen's Party and grew to include other unions before being brutally crushed.[17]

Another violent labor uprising occurred on May 1, 1886, when the notorious Haymarket Square bombing provoked an anti-labor backlash in which union organizers were accused of terrorism.[18] That same year the American Federation of Labor (AFL) was founded under Samuel Gompers. The AFL became known for political caution and its preference for skilled workers as members.

In an effort to control the threat created by business monopolies, Congress passed the Sherman Antitrust Act in 1890, which banned any "combination . . . in restraint of trade or commerce." The law would also be used in court injunctions against strikes. (An injunction orders a stop to a defined activity, which is then said to be enjoined.[19]) Two years later, in 1892, the Homestead Strike demonstrated just how fierce the battle between labor and business had become. Locked-out union steelworkers defeated steel magnate Andrew Carnegie's force of Pinkerton detectives in a shooting battle that killed 16 people. After the state militia arrived, the strike was broken, but not before both sides were shamed by the violence.[20] A less violent strike occurred that same year when unions made up of black and white members cooperated in a successful New Orleans general strike for a 10-hour day, overtime pay, and hiring preference for union members.

In 1893, the Illinois Women's Alliance, a coalition including AFL-associated socialist Elizabeth Morgan and Chicago reformer Jane Addams, won passage of the Factory Inspection Act, which prohibited factory labor under the age of 14 and created an eight-hour day for women and teenagers. A year later, in 1894, the American Railway Union's (ARU) Pullman Strike spread from Chicago to paralyze most of the U.S. rail system, then the lifeblood of interstate commerce. (The AFL refused to join.) Federal troops and state militiamen killed more than 50 strikers and rioters in seven states. Following the railway strike, the U.S. Supreme Court upheld federal criminal convictions of Eugene Debs and other ARU leaders for violating an injunction against interference with U.S. mail delivery. The decision encouraged more anti-labor court injunctions.[21]

One of the first notable court decisions of the twentieth century pertaining to labor came in 1905, when the U.S. Supreme Court ruled in *Lochner v. People of State of New York* that a state law restricting bakers' work to 60 hours per week and 10 hours per day violated the bakers' own right to freedom of contract.[22] That same year, Eugene Debs, William ("Big Bill") Haywood, Mary ("Mother") Jones, and others founded the radical International Workers of the World (IWW) with the desire to create "One Big Union" that would protect all workers. In 1906, three labor leaders, including Haywood, were tried for conspiracy to murder the former governor of Idaho, but were acquitted amid nationwide publicity.[23]

Deplorable working conditions received considerable exposure in 1906 with the publication of Upton Sinclair's *The Jungle*, a protest novel about Chicago meatpacking workers, which helped move public opinion toward regulating industry.[24] Then on March 25, 1911, a fire at the Triangle Shirtwaist Company in New York City, previously the site of a major strike, killed 146 workers. The victims were mostly young women, working on the upper floors of a 10-story building in which the exit doors were kept locked. Resulting anger promoted garment industry unions and new safety agreements.[25]

A year later, in 1912, textile (fiber, cloth, and clothing) workers in Lawrence, Massachusetts, went on strike to demand the same or better per-week pay after a state law reduced their working hours to 54 per week. An IWW-led citywide strike won better contracts for the striking workers, but the IWW was sidelined by political backlash.[26]

At the same time that the bloody battles of World War I (1914–1918) were being fought in Europe, unions were waging their own battles at home. In 1914, militiamen of the Colorado National Guard killed about 25 strikers in the Ludlow Massacre, which began the vicious final battles of the Colorado Coalfield War.[27] However, later that same year, the Clayton Act barred several kinds of antiunion injunctions (court orders), which was considered a major victory for the unions.[28] Then, in 1915, the labor movement suffered a serious setback when IWW leader and songwriter Joe Hill was executed after a controversial murder conviction.[29] On July 12, 1917, deputized antiunion vigilantes rounded up 1,186 actual and suspected IWW members in the Arizona mining town of Bisbee, forced them onto boxcars, and abandoned them in the New Mexican desert.[30]

Following the end of World War I, union supporters were accused of disloyalty and frequently imprisoned, in part because of fears stemming from the Bolshevik Revolution in Russia in 1917, which had removed the czar from power and established a communist government. During the 1920s, in a postwar antilabor backlash, U.S. courts again issued frequent antiunion injunctions, defeating the purpose of the Clayton Act.[31] Despite this, the all-black staff of Pullman passenger trains formed the Brotherhood of Sleeping Car Porters under A. Philip Randolph in 1925.[32]

After the stock market crash in 1929 and the start of the resulting Great Depression, the political winds again began to favor organized labor. In 1932, Congress passed the Norris-LaGuardia Act, which banned most antiunion court injunctions and other practices such as "yellow dog" contracts (agreements not to join unions).[33] In 1933, Congress passed the National Industrial Recovery Act (NIRA), which included protections of the right to join and organize unions.[34] Labor groups gained enough support to hold general strikes that shut down San Francisco, Minneapolis, and Toledo, Ohio, in 1934.[35] A year later, in 1935, the Committee for Industrial Organization (CIO, later the Congress of Industrial Organizations) left the AFL to pursue an "industrial" organizing approach to larger, less-skilled groups of workers, as opposed to the AFL's focus on skilled "craft" workers. Led by John L. Lewis and his United Mine Workers, the breakaways included several textile unions.

When the U.S. Supreme Court found the NIRA unconstitutional in 1935, Congress passed the National Labor Relations Act (NLRA or "Wagner Act"), with many of the same labor protections, although without protections for farm workers or against discrimination. Following this legislation, union membership began to rise before peaking in the mid-1950s.[36]

Summary

We may be at a turning point in U.S. labor history. Unions spent many years outside the power structure and sometimes outside the law. They gained insider status in the middle of the twentieth century, but their membership and power declined from the 1950s until recently. Now unions and pro-labor political ideas are gaining popularity again. However, the hard times that can make unions' arguments persuasive could hurt both labor and management.

Unions Are
Good For Society

"Eight hours for work, eight hours for rest, eight hours for what we will." This was a radical slogan once. It was shocking for people with money to think that people without money would claim two-thirds of each day for themselves.

Unions helped to establish weekends off and an eight-hour workday. Congress and state legislatures began officially requiring the eight-hour day as early as the 1860s, but they did not enforce it.[1] During the Great Depression, Congress passed the enforceable Fair Labor Standards Act of 1938, which established 40 hours as the standard workweek, with time-and-a-half overtime pay beyond 40 hours.[2]

It took more than a hundred years of campaigns to achieve the eight-hour day and two-day weekend, years of meetings, protests, speeches, and frequently bloody strikes.[3] A few ideas had to gain strength, radical ideas that are still not fully accepted:

nobody owns a permanent right to anyone else's work; everyone who performs work should be paid; the proper length for a day's work is the public's business; a full-time wage should be enough to live on; all people are entitled to the equal protection of the laws; and citizens still have rights as workers. The labor movement is necessary to promote and maintain workers' rights.

Unions reduce both injustice and radical reactions to it.

Before unions became fully legal, working people's lives were frequently hellish. Unions were necessary responses to the Industrial Revolution, the introduction of large-scale manufacturing that began in northwestern Europe in the mid-eighteenth century. One 1908 report estimated that each year industrial accidents were killing 30,000 to 35,000 U.S. male workers age 15 and older, out of about 26 million such workers then in the country, or more than 1.13 death per 1,000 workers.[4] By comparison, the official count of fatal U.S. work injuries in 2007 was 5,488, which is 3.7 per 100,000 workers.[5]

Before unions were legalized, organized labor actions such as strikes were frequently treated as criminal. It took courage or overwhelming strength in numbers for a powerless person like a factory worker to join a union. Those conditions encouraged the radical ideas of socialism and anarchism to flourish far more than in the safer labor movement of today. The big employers had radical ideas, too. In an 1887 speech, the year after the Haymarket bombing, the steel industrialist Andrew Carnegie announced to would-be radicals: "If you want to live in this country you must be quiet citizens or quiet corpses. That you may understand this we have hanged a few of your fellows and if you don't observe that intimation we will hang more of you."[6]

Legalized unions make society safer, more stable, and more just because they can speak for people who would otherwise feel powerless. When people feel unrepresented, they can become angry in unmanageable ways. Just as citizens of a country should have a say in its governance, they should also have rights in the workplace.

The bad old days have not ended while unions are weak.

Horrible conditions still exist in industries and places where unions are difficult to form. There are continuing reports of labor abuses involving Asian immigrants to Saipan, a U.S. possession in the Northern Mariana Islands where many clothing companies have factories. Describing one fact-finding trip to Saipan, Senator Lisa Murkowski (R-Alaska) said the investigators met people who

> sometimes faced the problems found in classic company towns that we would have found in America's Wild West. Situations where workers were paid, [then] forced to pay much of their low wages for their room and their board, having to work off recruitment fees before they could change their jobs. Additionally, there were workers who would not get paid for months on end, who ended up in unsafe working conditions and in some cases were coerced into prostitution, or into having abortions so that they could continue to work without interruption.[7]

THE LETTER OF THE LAW

The National Labor Relations Act, 29 U.S. Code, Section 7, as passed in 1935 as Public Law 74-198

Employees shall have the right to self-organization, to form, join, or assist labor organizations, to bargain collectively through representatives of their own choosing, and to engage in other concerted activities for the purpose of collective bargaining or other mutual aid or protection.

In recent years there have also been terrible stories of child labor and near-slavery conditions among immigrant farm workers and guest workers within the United States.[8]

Some people might say stories about immigrants or people in Saipan have little to do with the average American worker, but they would be ignoring settled patterns in American labor history. The worst-treated workers in the United States have always been those viewed as foreign or inferior. Their wages have always defined the "floor" of the labor market. Through the nineteenth and early twentieth centuries, many employers, as well as some unions, profited by treating many people as inferior and debasing their wage rates accordingly, mainly anyone who was not an American-born, English-speaking protestant male of North European (non-Irish) ancestry.[9] Beginning in the 1880s, the better minds of the labor movement began to see that anyone's lower wage undercuts everyone's pay rate, so it was best for unions to include everyone. As an old union slogan has it, "an injury to one is an injury to all."

Within the United States today, workers are badly treated in industries such as home care, retail sales, and fast food, where unions are hard to organize, wages are low, and workforces are transient. Employment in these industries is usually "at will," meaning either side can end the relationship at any time. This may seem like freedom except that people who can always be fired have to be afraid of any risk or change, either at work or at home. Barbara Ehrenreich, a journalist who went undercover to write about low-wage jobs, concludes, "When you enter the low-wage workplace—and many of the medium-wage workplaces as well—you check your civil liberties at the door, leave America and all it supposedly stands for behind, and learn to zip your lips for the duration of the shift."[10]

Union members are not strangers. They're us.

Corporate antiunion rhetoric sometimes invites people to think of themselves as "consumers," and implies that their main economic interest should be in finding bargains. This approach suggests that employees who ask for higher pay are opponents of consumers, who should want businesses to have low labor costs and therefore low prices. Except that the people who are asking for higher wages are not greedy strangers—they are us.

Despite the decline in membership in recent decades, there are still millions of union members. In early 2009, there were an estimated 306 million people in the United States.[11] In 2008, the United States had 129,377,000 employed people over 16 years old, of whom 16,098,000 were union members.[12]

Most consumers depend on their own or someone else's wages for shopping money. As of 2008, workers with union representation earned median wages of $886 per week while the median for nonunion workers was only $691.[13] That means every time a union job disappears, somebody has about $800 less per month to take to the mall, the grocery store, or the car dealership.

Unions are accused of harming the economy by raising business costs. However, a business that underpays its staff, even if it also charges low prices, drafts its employees into the "race to the bottom." That is, it forces people with small paychecks to look for the cheapest prices, even if they would rather not take advantage of others' underpaid labor.[14]

A popular theory suggests ordinary Americans are more likely than ordinary people in other countries to expect they might one day become the boss, which makes Americans generally less likely to join unions and more sympathetic to owners and employers. This is sometimes called the Horatio Alger myth, named after a nineteenth-century writer of popular novels about poor boys who impress rich benefactors and become important men.[15] While the United States does indeed produce "rags-to-riches" stories, it also produces lottery winners—and yet few people invest their savings in lottery tickets! The opposite idea, that most people are stuck at their current economic level, may seem depressing. It can, however, lead people to recognize that many Americans are in the same boat, and to form unions that improve life for everyone, not just for a few.

The middle class depends on unions.

Once upon a time in the upper Midwest, a male General Motors assembly worker's job in the 1950s could pay not only for a suburban house and two cars, but living expenses for his wife and children, college for the children later on, and a summer cottage on a northern lake. That was once understood as an ordinary middle-class standard of living in the United States of America. Not everyone got that life, but large numbers of people did and, as the civil rights movements began, the nation could hope that everyone might join that middle class someday. Today, few people can live in the American middle class on factory wages.

Whole libraries of academic writing praise the value of a middle class. Middle-class people are not too tired or worried or ill to plan for the future. They make good citizens because they get involved in local politics and educate their children. Unions helped to create a thriving middle class in the United States.

In the last two generations, as unions lost power, working Americans' standard of living fell and inequality grew. Roughly speaking, when union membership rises, inequality falls; when union membership falls, inequality rises. Inequality, measured as the percentage of all income received by the top 10 percent of Americans, was high before the mid-1930s and union membership was low. In the late 1930s and early 1940s, inequality plunged as union membership increased. Then inequality crept downward while union membership rose into the 1950s. From the 1950s until the last few years, inequality rose while union membership slipped downward. In recent years, union membership has begun to rise again, while inequality figures have wavered since about 2002.

Unions fight the "race to the bottom."

The term "race to the bottom" describes the harm done when businesses compete with each other to cut costs. In particular, manufacturing businesses tend to move jobs where workers can be paid the least—for example, to countries where it is illegal to

Union Membership and Inequality Statistics

One of the best union membership graphs available, for 1930 through 2003, is in Gerald Mayer's "Union Membership Trends in the United States," Congressional Research Service, 2004, at http://digitalcommons.ilr.cornell.edu/cgi/viewcontent. cgi?article=1176&context=key_workplace.

Other sources include the Bureau of Labor Statistics "Employment Cost Trends" page at http://www.bls.gov/ect/, and an academic site, "Unionstats," at http:// unionstats.gsu.edu/. For some earlier figures see the Economic History Services site, at http://eh.net/databases/labor/.

Some inequality figures are available on the U.S. Census Bureau's "Income" page at http://www.census.gov/hhes/www/income/income.html. See especially Arthur F. Jones Jr. and Daniel H. Weinberg, "The Changing Shape of the Nation's Income Distribution 1947–1998," *Current Population Reports*, June 2000, at http://www. census.gov/prod/2000pubs/p60-204.pdf.

Professor Emmanuel Saez of the University of California at Berkeley and Professor Thomas Piketty of the Paris School of Economics have developed long-term estimates of income and inequality in the United States and other countries, many of which are available at http://elsa.berkeley.edu/~saez/. See especially, "Striking It Richer," at http://elsa.berkeley.edu/~saez/saez-UStopincomes-2006prel.pdf. Alan Reynolds of the conservative/libertarian Cato Institute criticized these figures in "The Top 1%... of What?" *Wall Street Journal*, Dec. 14, 2006, http://online.wsj. com/article/SB116607104815649971.html?mod=opinion_main_commentaries. The professors' response to these criticisms may be found at http://elsa.berkeley. edu/~saez/answer-WSJreynolds.pdf.

The Bureau of Labor Statistics Inflation Calculator, at http://data.bls.gov/cgi-bin/cpicalc.pl, may help you compare figures. For example, it uses the consumer price index to compute that a wage of $1.00 per hour in 1950 had the same buying power as $8.93 per hour in 2008.

join an independent union. When not restrained by law or contract, business owners may feel that competition forces them to move jobs in this way even if presumably they would rather not hurt their existing workers.

In fact, some of the manufacturing jobs that left the northern United States in the 1970s and 1980s have been traveling the world ever since as company owners continue to look for places with cheaper labor. First stop was the American South, with its antiunion right-to-work laws. As of 2008, all the states with union membership below 5 percent were southern. Incomes are no longer uniformly lower in the South, which they were around 1950, but the highest statewide average wages are still elsewhere in the nation.[16]

Next came "maquiladora" factories just over the Mexican border. These are factories that import needed equipment and materials on a duty-free and tariff-free basis, assemble or manufacture the goods there, and then export them back to the originating country. A 2000 study sponsored by labor and activist groups found that in 15 maquiladora cities, "it would take between four and five minimum wage salaries to meet the basic needs of a family of four."[17]

China followed Mexico. Chinese work circumstances vary, but some are terrible. Despite efforts of corporations to avoid sending work to places with the worst conditions, inspections may miss problems that a factory owner is determined to hide.[18] Poor safety standards kill Chinese workers at rates not seen in America for a hundred years. For example, in February 2009, 74 miners died in a single coal mine explosion, and the Chinese government reported about 3,200 deaths in mining accidents during 2008.[19]

As strong demand for labor in China has lifted some wages, Vietnamese labor has been found to be even cheaper. The *New York Times* reported in 2006, "While Chinese wages are still less than $1 an hour, factory workers in Vietnam earn as little as $50 a month for a 48-hour workweek, including Saturdays."[20]

Unions make and maintain institutions that protect everyone.

Some people claim that unions are unnecessary now because U.S. government agencies protect things like minimum wages, maximum hours, pensions, health insurance funds, and consumer and workplace safety. Yet unions helped create those protective agencies and are needed to defend them. Some scholars say unions have been better at passing laws to protect the general public than at passing laws to protect their own right to organize.[21] In this view, people who believe they can do without unions are riding free at union members' expense.

The need for unions can also be understood by looking around a specific American workplace, especially one with lower-paid employees. How often are all those helpful-sounding rules enforced? How can they be, when one study found that, from 1975 to 2004, the Department of Labor reduced its number of wage and hour investigators?[22]

Some employers will claim they do not need unions to tell them to treat workers well. Such a claim cannot be tested unless unionization is possible. A nonunion employer who "doesn't need unions" still knows unions exist, and may be trying to keep workers happy so they will not join one. When someone earns a higher wage than peers in a similar job, it raises the pay standards in a whole industry, so nonunion people benefit from a union contract as well. Solidarity—the virtue of sticking together for the common good—has to start somewhere, or the unrestrained market will reduce nearly everyone to a short life of long work hours at subsistence wages.

It takes unions to make sure the laws already on the books are enforced. It takes unions to kick up a fuss under federal law when a company's pension fund shrinks. It takes unions to create and maintain assumptions about what is normal and moral behavior in a workplace on days when the government inspector does not visit. Although some nonprofit organizations campaign for things like workplace and consumer safety, they may see what they do as charity, or helping the unfortunate. Nonprofits may fail, lose funding, or change focus. People in a workplace still need to work together through unions to stand up for themselves without waiting to be rescued from above.

Summary

Unions brought you the weekend and the middle class. Unions helped create civil rights laws and the protective government agencies that people point to when they claim that unions are no longer necessary. Where unions lose power, inequality and other forms of injustice flourish. It is destructive for the economy as a whole to allow businesses to join the "race to the bottom" for lower labor costs because low-paid people cannot afford to spend money to keep the economy flourishing. Although other groups and the government also protect rights, nothing can replace unions.

Unions Harm Society as a Whole

Pro-union rhetoric can succeed by using black-and-white arguments, by claiming that employees are good and employers bad, but it does not help an antiunion case to argue the opposite. It is more effective to note that, although employers want to assert their rights, they do treat employees better than unions would like to admit—and that union leaders are more selfish than their members might like to think. Most antiunion political players now assert support for basic labor rights. For example, the U.S. Chamber of Commerce, which uniformly campaigns to limit union power, states that it "strongly supports the right of workers to voluntarily join unions under fair and democratic rules."[1]

"Big Labor" is real—and still ugly.

From an antiunion perspective, labor got ugly, then it got big and ugly. A wild period in labor history began in the 1870s, following the Civil War. As previously noted, many events in the history of labor between the Civil War and World War I involved violence, not just one-sided attacks on virtuous protesters, but instances of fierce mutual combat. Labor's violent tendencies still exist, although a more thoroughly policed society has restrained them.

Historian Thaddeus Russell provides an account of Jimmy Hoffa's Detroit Teamsters in the 1930s that sounds more like gang warfare than collective bargaining. Russell suggests the Teamsters got along well with gangsters and ex-smugglers left over from Prohibition—the national ban on the sale, manufacture, and transportation of alcohol for consumption in the United States from 1920 to 1933. According to Russell, from the 1930s into the 1950s, the Teamsters would "organize" workplaces by threatening their owners, either with direct harm or with the loss of deliveries and business partners. He describes how Hoffa's Local 299 (a local union chartered by the International Brotherhood of Teamsters) "organized" companies that delivered new cars:

> Rather than devoting their time to signing up workers and petitioning for representation elections, they preferred a two-step strategy that was far more effective. . . . The local's business agents first approached the owner of a firm and told him that if he did not enroll his employees with the union his trucks would be bombed. Next, if the employer refused to capitulate, they bombed his trucks.[2]

Because of stories like these, Congress made it illegal for unions to pressure a nonunion employer through its customers or suppliers. Union language may call such behavior "solidarity" or a "sympathy strike," but in federal law these are illegal "secondary" tactics. A nonviolent example of a "secondary strike" would be if workers at an auto assembly plant walked out to protest the use of parts from a nonunion plant. If they stayed at work but refused to handle the nonunion parts, that would be a "secondary boycott." Pro-union workers from the parts plant would engage in "secondary picketing" if they carried signs outside the main assembly plant advocating a "secondary boycott" through messages such as "Don't Buy Nonunion Parts." Such practices were partly banned by the 1947 Taft-Hartley Act and completely banned by the 1959 Landrum-Griffin Act.[3]

By the 1950s, the combination of an illicit past and 20 years of legal unionizing had turned some union leaderships into selfish, gangster-like bureaucracies. Some liberal and leftwing historians argue that leftist union members were a counterweight to corruption and greed until union leftists lost power in the 1940s and 1950s. They argue that when anticommunist congressional hearings and new federal laws forced alleged and real communists to give up union leadership, control rested with dull pragmatists who cared mostly about contract terms. (The antiunion sentiment and anticommunism of the era are among reasons cited why the American Federation of Labor, then led by George Meany and the Congress of Industrial Organizations under Walter Reuther of the United Auto Workers, joined to form the AFL-CIO with Meany as president.) This does not, however, change the fact that union leaders had, by the 1950s, become political insiders, as powerful as many of the owners and employers they were bargaining with.[4]

A new political type emerged: the power-hungry "labor boss." In the hard times of the 1930s, unions had held some moral high ground. By the 1950s, however, the labor boss became an equally unattractive counterpart to the old stereotype of the greedy factory owner. To ordinary citizens, such leaders seemed to deserve each other, especially in light of the fact that, as historian Nelson Lichtenstein notes, "the civil rights movement had begun to stir, which set a new and higher standard for those who claimed to speak for the underdog."[5]

In fact, unions had acquired enough power to cause a national security crisis. In April 1952, President Harry Truman ordered a government seizure of steel mills to prevent an ongoing

Well-Armored Think Tanks

Pro-union and antiunion perspectives have supporters among Washington lobbying groups and "think tanks," meaning organizations or institutes that conduct research and serve as advocates for various fields.

Pro-union lobbying groups include the major unions themselves, which now have extensive research and legislative arms. Pro-union think tanks include the Center for American Progress (http://www.americanprogress.org); the Economic Policy Institute (http://www.epi.org); and the Urban Institute (http://www.urban.org).

Prominent antiunion lobbying groups include the U.S. Chamber of Commerce (http://www.uschamber.com); the National Right to Work Committee (http://www.right-to-work.org) and its sister organization, the National Right to Work Legal Defense Foundation (http://www.nrtw.org); the Associated Builders and Contractors (http://www.abc.org), the National Association of Manufacturers (http://www.nam.org), and the National Federation of Independent Business (http://www.nfib.com).

Antiunion think tanks include the Heritage Institute (http://www.heritage.org) and the Michigan-based Mackinac Center for Public Policy (http://www.mackinac.org). The Cato Institute (http://www.cato.org) opposes unions on libertarian grounds, because it believes in maximizing individual liberty and minimizing the amount of state influence on citizens.

The projects of political consultant Richard Berman form a category of their own. Berman's company maintains Web sites for the antiunion Center for Union Facts (http://www.UnionFacts.com), the Employee Freedom Action Committee (http://www.employeefreedom.org), the Employment Policies Institute (http://www.epionline.org), and related sites, including http://www.laborpains.org and http://www.teachersunionexposed.com.

The AFL-CIO and others attack these sites as mere fronts for groups that lack grassroots membership. (Search "Berman" at http://www.afl-cio.org.) A liberal-funded group, Citizens for Responsibility and Ethics in Washington or CREW (http://www.citizensforethics.org), maintains a whole anti-Berman Web site (http://www.bermanexposed.org).

Sources: Web sites cited above and Jim VandeHei and Chris Cillizza, "A New Alliance Of Democrats Spreads Funding," *Washington Post*, July 17, 2006, http://www.washingtonpost.com/wp-dyn/content/article/2006/07/16/AR2006071600882_pf.html.

Jimmy Hoffa, president of the International Brotherhood of Teamsters, points to a paper held by Robert F. Kennedy, counsel of the Senate Labor Rackets Committee, as he speaks to Kennedy in the committee's hearing room on September 17, 1958.

labor dispute with the United Steelworkers from halting production for the Korean War (1950–1953).[6]

By the mid-1950s, public opinion was turning sharply against what was starting to be called "Big Labor." In the 1954 film *On the Waterfront*, Marlon Brando starred as an ex-prizefighter who takes a stand against union corruption on the New York docks. The film implied similarities between labor organizations and communism in their suppression of the individual and their hatred of informers. (The film's director, Elia Kazan, had recently provided the names of associates from his days as a member of the U.S. Communist Party to the House Un-American Actvities

Committee, an investigative committee of the U.S. House of Representatives determined to stop the spread of communism.) Russell wrote, "Millions of Americans admired the film for exposing the tyranny of corrupt labor unions over helpless workers and providing a compelling tale of good triumphing over evil."[7]

Then, beginning in 1957 and lasting nearly three years, a special committee of the U.S. Senate held televised hearings on labor corruption, particularly in the Teamsters. The leading questioner for the McClellan Committee was Robert F. Kennedy, the future attorney general and senator from New York, who was then a Senate attorney fresh from service in the anticommunist hearings.[8]

Millions of Americans with new television sets watched as Teamsters official Jimmy Hoffa, Teamsters President Dave

QUOTABLE

Robert F. Kennedy v. Jimmy Hoffa

During the McClellan Committee hearings in August 1957, Senate attorney Robert Kennedy and committee members, including the panel's chairman, Senator John L. McClellan, D-Ark., questioned Jimmy Hoffa, then a vice president of the International Brotherhood of Teamsters. Among other charges, they accused Hoffa of trying to line up Teamsters union charters (memberships) for some locals of other unions that were in trouble with their parent organizations for corruption. Here they discussed Hoffa's contacts with John "Johnny Dio" Dioguardi, head of a United Auto Workers (UAW) local. Dioguardi had been indicted on tax evasion charges in April 1953, in part because he allegedly took an employer's payoff to *prevent* unionization at a plant in Allentown, Pennsylvania. This was the logical extreme of a more common alleged corrupt practice: negotiating "sweetheart" contracts that helped employers and union officers at members' expense. Here, Hoffa ducked questions about Dioguardi's record:

The Chairman: Mr. Hoffa, the information counsel gave you about Dio's indictment was published in the *New York Times*, with Dio's picture, on April

Beck, and others testified. They heard about corrupt personal uses of union money, union involvement in organized crime, and routine violence. While the hearings continued, Hoffa became president of the Teamsters, and the AFL-CIO expelled the Teamsters for corruption. Hoffa was arrested but acquitted in the first of several federal prosecutions.[9] The public's support for unions began to fall, and not just among political conservatives. (Hoffa was eventually convicted of federal jury tampering and fraud in 1964. He began a 13-year prison sentence in 1967 but was released in 1971 after appealing to President Richard Nixon for clemency. In 1975, he disappeared, presumed murdered by associates in organized crime.[10])

The stink created by the exposure of union corruption in the 1950s still sticks to labor even after the AFL-CIO parted ways

23, 15 days before your meeting. It is bound to have been called to your attention at that time. Do you say you did not know that?

Mr. Hoffa: No, sir; I did not. I said I knew that he was indicted for income tax.

Mr. Kennedy: Did you know anything else about him? Did you know that he had been convicted of extortion in 1937 and had been in Sing Sing?

Mr. Hoffa: I think that earlier in the discussion I said I learned, whether or not it was that time or later, that he had been.

Mr. Kennedy: And the hiring of Benny the Bug, his hiring of Joe Curcio with a police record, Abe Goldberg; and that he had been denounced for running a racket union; that the district attorney had denounced him in 1952 for running a racket union; that the AFL had charged him with racketeering; all of these things prior to the time that you are having these conversations with him and meeting with him?

(The witness conferred with his counsel.)

Source: Senate Hearings, Select Committee on Improper Activities in the Labor or Management Field, Part 35, 85th Cong., 2d Sess., August 20, 21, 22 and 23, 1957, Part 13. U.S. GPO, 1957, pp. 5196–5198: http://www.archive.org/details/investigationofi13unit.

with the Teamsters. Some leaders of other unions, like United Auto Workers chief Walter Reuther, attempted to rebuild their images by conducting their own drives against corruption.[11] Although this happened half a century ago, it seems as if some unions have simply become smaller, older versions of what they were in the 1950s, without reforming or moving on. Many people believe the new unions are no more attractive than the old ones. Where the old guard was corrupt but predictable, the new group could renew some of the disruptive tactics that hurt businesses before Taft-Hartley.

Unions slow economic growth.

Unions are bad for business growth, and thus for the economy in general, even if they help individual members. For example, economist Barry T. Hirsch writes:

> There has been extensive study in recent years, particularly in the U.S., of the relationship of unionization to productivity, profitability, investment, and employment growth. The broad pattern that emerges from these studies is that unions significantly increase compensation for their members, but fail to increase productivity sufficiently to offset the cost increases from higher compensation. As a result, unions are associated with lower profitability, decreased investment in physical capital and research and development (R&D), and lower rates of employment and sales growth.[12]

That is, individual union members may get paid more, but they slow down employers' ability to create new jobs.

Many who argue against unions claim it is foolish to focus on promoting economic equality because a more equal world is on average a poorer one. The U.S. Chamber of Commerce makes this argument in a series of "white papers" on unions for the general reader.[13] These papers advance the free-market theory supported by many conservatives that "a rising tide lifts all boats," meaning that a fast-growing economy, even with bigger differences between rich and poor, creates greater prosperity for all. One paper cites research that claims unions reduced the U.S. gross domestic product, an important measure of economic productivity, by as much as $3.5 trillion between 1947 and 2000, and also quotes a different group of researchers who found greater productivity and faster job growth in less unionized right-to-work states.

A separate Chamber of Commerce report contrasts pessimistic union rhetoric about the state of American working life with more encouraging material from government and think-tank sources. The report states that most people are reasonably happy with their jobs, that overall the U.S. median income, even adjusted for inflation, rose almost 30 percent from 1967 to 2007, and that complaints about losses in wages do not account for increases in benefits.[14]

Faith in the free market as an economic philosophy goes back to the "classical liberalism" of pioneering eighteenth-century economists like Adam Smith. (The term "liberal" here refers to liberalizing markets by lifting government restrictions, not to present-day political liberalism.) Smith's principles still underlie much of mainstream "neoclassical" economics. Such free-market philosophy contrasts with the ideas of John Maynard Keynes, who argued that governments should support economic demand by encouraging high employment at good wages so people have money to spend.[15] An economic emphasis on increasing business profit is sometimes called "supply-side economics" because it counts on businesses to invest those profits in creating more jobs and goods. (By contrast, Keynesian demand-side economics tries to drive the economy from the other side, by bringing buyers more money to spend.) "Neoconservatism" refers to a modernized style of conservatism that, from the 1960s onward, has put forward free-market doctrines while reducing emphasis on small-town social conservatism. A third term, "Neoliberalism" combines liberalism in the modern sense on social issues with free-market answers to economic problems.[16] For example, although the Clinton administration supported unions, its approach to economic policy was mostly based on faith in free markets. (During the 1990s, "neoliberalism" was used internationally and among U.S. leftists to describe policies favoring the largest businesses; overseas it has connotations associated in the U.S. with "neoconservatism.")

According to free-market economic theory, the world economy suffers if business owners are forced to operate in places where pro-union laws and organizations raise labor costs. A manufacturing employer who cannot afford to pay factory workers $30 per hour may have to move a factory somewhere with lower wages to stay in business at all. Supporters of free markets often accuse unions of unfair "protectionism," of trying to freeze job situations in places that no longer fit into the world's changing economy. While pro-union arguments regarding the human cost of the "race to the bottom" often seem persuasive, they fail to address the fact that it is wrong to assume life is always worse in lower-wage places, since the cost of living is often lower in such places too.[17] In addition, it may be argued that union supporters contribute to poverty by holding back economic growth that could employ more people everywhere.

Critics of unions also contend that it shows regional or national prejudice to claim there is less respect for workers' lives and dignity in lower-wage places; for example, to think of China as one gigantic sweatshop. The U.S. entrepreneur and tech wizard Andrew "Bunnie" Huang told an interviewer that although he found many toy factory conditions "awful," he was satisfied with the factories that made his Internet music/display/clock gadget, the Chumby. He said he made a point of staying in the factory workers' dormitories and eating their food:

I mean there's things that guys can do still in China to sort of fool me. Like they have a special day when they know I'm coming to the floor and they'll give them extra special food or something. That's happened before. But generally speaking, I like to make sure that the conditions are good. And I sleep well at night knowing that we build Chumby in factories where people are actually fairly well taken care of, right?[18]

The phrase "we pass the savings on to you" tells a real truth. If all products sold in the United States were made at the prevailing U.S. union wages, prices would become unaffordable to many Americans. The libertarian Cato Institute estimates that

Really? $70 an hour?

How high are manufacturing labor costs in unionized places and industries? A 2008 report from the conservative think tank the Heritage Foundation stated that UAW union members in the Big Three auto plants cost their employers "over $70 an hour in wages and current and future benefits." The $70 figure covers benefits and taxes as well as the paychecks workers receive, and not just current workers' own benefits. It divides the hours being worked by current employees into all the benefits being paid, including to retirees, which means an individual worker is not getting a full $70 per hour in any form. (The auto employers do have to keep paying the pensions to comply with their side of the contracts that keep current employees working.) But how high are the actual wages anyway? As of 2007, an average of $28 per hour, sometimes more, which is still pretty good money and higher than that of nonunion employers.

Sources: James Sherk, "UAW Workers Actually Cost the Big Three Automakers $70 an Hour," WebMemo #2162, Heritage Foundation; http://www.heritage.org/Research/Economy/wm2162.cfm. Jonathan Cohn, "Debunking the Myth of the $70-per-hour Autoworker," *New Republic*, Nov. 21, 2008; http://www.tnr.com/politics/story.html?id=1026e955-541c-4aa6-bcf2-56dfc3323682.

"[t]he offshoring of computer-related manufacturing jobs has accounted for 10% to 30% of the drop in hardware prices." Cato's Daniel Ikenson recently argued that "Buy American" provisions in the early-2009 economic recovery proposals "would mean higher price tags, fewer projects funded, and fewer people hired."[19]

Unions are unnecessary.

Employment rights have made progress over the past hundred years, and unions cannot claim all the credit. Employers have economic and moral reasons to treat employees well voluntarily. Good employers have been providing for employees for a long time. Some attempts to do so, such as company towns (entire communities centered around a factory or mine), have had undesirable effects, but there is a good side to welfare capitalism (the business practice of providing benefits such as medical care, pensions, and other perks) for the mutual benefit of employers and employees.

During the 1920s, even as union power receded, steel companies expanded employee benefits. Judge Elbert Gary of U.S. Steel "explained to U.S. Steel's stockholders that expenditures of $10 million a year for employee welfare were necessary 'because it is the way men ought to be treated, and secondly because it pays to treat men in that way.'" True, U.S. Steel kept the 12-hour workday until 1923, but the workers received pension and savings plans and medical care as part of their employment.[20] In another example, the Kaiser Permanente health plan, still a major health maintenance organization, was founded by Henry J. Kaiser to serve employees of his West Coast construction and shipyard work sites during the 1940s.[21]

Pensions, health insurance, workplace safety, employee input, and consumer protection are in the interest of employers and governments, and they would be even without unions. Most owners want to keep their employees healthy and happy. Employers and their insurance companies have to pay for accidents or violations of rights. An owner who is responsible for a business cannot afford to let a union run it, but must balance what is in the best interest of his or her business against the needs of employees.

Additionally, unions may be less needed now that government agencies regulate the workplaces and workers can file complaints or lawsuits if they feel mistreated. For example, as previously noted, fatal work accident rates fell dramatically between 1908 and 2007, in large part due to government oversight. The lowest fatal accident rate ever on record was in 2007,[22] which was also the second-lowest year for union membership since unions were legalized. That means employers and regulators did not need strong unions to make them reduce risks. For example, the federal Occupational Safety and Health Administration (OSHA), created in 1970, now enforces safety laws in both union and nonunion workplaces.[23]

Workers can now defend their rights directly, as individuals, without the need for unionization. The pro-union labor historian Nelson Lichtenstein argues that the workplace civil rights achievements of the late twentieth century created a major new thread in labor history. Individuals complaining of mistreatment, especially illegal discrimination, have established new standards by appealing directly to the courts.

Summary

Union supporters often divide the world into two opposing sides, employers and employees, but critics of unions must demonstrate that labor issues are not simple right and wrong issues. The widespread corruption exposed in the congressional hearings of the 1950s shows that unions are not all good. Even though the 1950s were a long time ago, some bad habits remain in modern unions. Although unions may raise some people's wages, they can also slow economic growth. Finally, unions have made themselves unnecessary thanks to laws that protect all workers as individuals.

Current Labor Laws Favor Employers

S ay you want to start a union at your office. You have just learned that some male coworkers who drink with the boss after work are getting higher pay than women in similar jobs. You and some friends meet with a union business agent on your lunch hour. The business agent asks some questions to see if it is worth committing an organizer. How many of your coworkers are angry enough to organize? Would there be enough employees with the same interests to create a bargaining unit for union representation? How many employees are supervisors who are not permitted to join a union? Do you realize you could get fired for organizing, then wait years just for a decision as to whether the firing was illegal? Do you understand how much paperwork a union election takes? The business agent sighs and says, "Look, if there's pay discrimination, maybe you should just file a civil rights complaint."

There are too many restrictions on organizing.

The AFL-CIO says people join unions when they have the chance but that many cannot because the law makes it difficult for people to form a union without getting fired first.[1] The rules of the game were far different during the greatest period of union growth, from passage of the Wagner Act in 1935 until passage of the Taft-Hartley Act in 1947. Unions had campaigned for more than a century to get the advantages they enjoyed during those 12 years.

Courts routinely blocked union activity from the 1880s until the Great Depression. Congress protected unions against most court injunctions with the Norris-LaGuardia Act of 1932, then established the right to join and organize unions with the National Industrial Recovery Act in 1933. After that measure was found unconstitutional on other grounds, Congress substituted the National Labor Relations Act (NLRA, also known as the Wagner Act) in 1935.[2] The Supreme Court upheld the NLRA in the 1937 case of *NLRB v. Jones & Laughlin Steel Corp.*,[3] which confirmed that the National Labor Relations Board (NLRB) could stop a steel plant from firing employees for union activity and could order the plant to rehire those it had already fired. Following this decision, union membership rose.

As unions gained power and influence, their images became less attractive. Assumptions changed in Congress from 1935 to 1959 about whom labor laws should defend. The NLRA presumed that the underdogs were employees facing stronger employers. The 1947 Labor Management Relations Act (the Taft-Hartley Act) saw unions and employers as fairly matched opponents that could each commit "unfair labor practices." The 1959 Landrum-Griffin Act portrayed employees as underdogs again, but this time menaced by their own unions. Landrum-Griffin included a "bill of rights" guaranteeing union members' rights, such as to speak freely at meetings and to review union financial records—a long way from the assumption in 1935 that unions represented their members.[4]

The Taft-Hartley Act bureaucratized and hobbled union organizing in the United States. President Harry Truman, although not especially predisposed to support unions, tried unsuccessfully to stop it with a veto.[5] The law added definitions of "unfair labor practices" by both labor and management to the NLRA and empowered the NLRB to judge and punish both. Today, the NLRB supervises the union recognition process, including elections for union representation, and investigates unfair labor practices. If, for example, you are fired for trying to start a union, you first have to complain to an NLRB regional office. The staff there may help you try to negotiate a settlement with the employer. If that fails to work, the NLRB staff may issue a formal complaint against the employer. An administrative law judge (ALJ) then holds a hearing on the complaint, while a representative of the NLRB general counsel's office serves as prosecutor. The ALJ issues a report on the hearing, which may become the NLRB's final decision on the matter unless the board chooses to consider it independently. If the NLRB does reach a decision on its own, it cannot enforce its order but must ask the federal courts to do so. So if you want your lost job back, you may have to accumulate support over a period of years from the NLRB's regional office staff, the ALJ, the full NLRB, a federal court, and a federal appeals court. If you win, the employer may have to pay you back wages, but by then the possibility of starting a union at your old workplace may have disappeared.

Because of Taft-Hartley restrictions, a union can no longer use secondary strikes or boycotts to pressure an employer through its business partners. For example, seamstresses trying to organize an obscure garment sweatshop are forbidden to picket the big-name department store that sells the dresses they make. Businesses harmed by illegal secondary tactics may sue the union responsible. Taft-Hartley also gives workers the right to cross a picket line and prohibits unions from stopping them. It bans "closed shop" agreements, which formerly could limit hiring to workers who were already union members. It does permit "union security" agreements, which allow an employer to hire people regardless of union status, provided the new hires quickly join the union or pay union dues.[6]

Taft-Hartley established a complex process that must be followed before an employer is required to recognize a union as its employees' representative. Employers may choose to recognize a union if a majority of their employees has signed cards or a petition in its support, but most employers choose not to. Typically they exercise their right to demand an election by secret ballot. The NLRB-supervised election process often takes long enough that the employer has time to frighten people away from voting union, secret ballot or not.

The board also asks endless, tricky questions about who belongs in each "bargaining unit." A bargaining unit contains employees, usually with similar job descriptions and sharing a "community of interest," who would be represented by the same union in negotiating the same contract. Managers and the people who work most closely with them are prohibited from membership in unions under the NLRA. These workers are considered to be professional employees and cannot be in bargaining units with nonprofessionals unless most of the professionals agree. Company security guards who enforce rules against employees cannot belong to the same union as those employees. Employers trying to break up a union's strength tend to push questions like whether senior hospital nurses count as supervisors or whether a manager's secretary is a "confidential" employee who cannot be a union member.[7]

Unions need more organizing protections.

In 2009, Congress was preparing to add worker protections to federal union recognition law for the first time since Taft-Hartley. However, it appeared legislative compromises might water down the originally proposed measures, disappointing unions. At issue was the Employee Free Choice Act (EFCA) proposal, which took the form of two bills before Congress, H.R.

1409 and S.560. During the 2008 presidential campaign and in the Obama administration's first days, discussion of the EFCA had focused on the bill's central provision at the time: "card check" union recognition.

"Card check" would require an employer to recognize a union, if more than half the bargaining unit members signed union authorization cards. Unions argue this would be simpler than the current election process, and fairer because it would not give employers the chance to intimidate employees before a vote. It would certainly make unionization easier. So much easier that employer groups campaigned against it fiercely in the 2008 elections, and a co-founder of Home Depot called it "the demise of civilization."[8] A Congressional Research Service report found "card check" recognition would get unions recognized sooner and more often, likely increasing wages overall, whereas a mandatory secret ballot would probably make union recognition less likely and might therefore lower wages.[9] In mid-2009, the *New York Times* reported that a bill with the EFCA name might be passed, but without the "card check" provision.

To see differences that either "card check" or the substitute EFCA proposals might make in union recognition, consider an incident in 2002, when workers at the Consolidated Biscuit factory in McComb, Ohio, wanted to unionize. Writer Esther Kaplan reported that "more than 650 of 800" workers signed cards expressing interest in a union. That's where the matter would have ended under the "card check" proposal. Under then-current law, it proved to be far more difficult. Kaplan writes that "after Consolidated Biscuit hired a unionbusting firm and started threatening workers with firings or deportations or shuttering the plant altogether, the union lost the election." In 2004, an ALJ with the NLRB found Consolidated Biscuit had broken the law in several ways, but did not change the results of the election. After administrative and court appeals, at least one man fired for organizing went back to work at the factory in December 2008.[10]

As the Consolidated Biscuit case shows, managers sometimes threaten people's jobs and futures to keep their employees

FROM THE BENCH

National Labor Relations Board v. Consolidated Biscuit Company, 6th District Court of Appeals (2008)

A federal appeals court found that James Appold, the president of the Consolidated Biscuit Company, had made illegal "coercive statements" during otherwise legal antiunion lectures at "captive audience" meetings for employees. In its decision, the appeals court wrote:

> Two or three days before the representation election, CBC held seven or eight employee meetings at which Appold spoke and Vice President Larry Ivan ran a slide projector. Nearly all of CBC's employees attended one of these meetings. Ivan testified that Appold told employees, "when you begin to bargain, you start from zero, you don't start from where you're at and bargain. Forward, from that point you start with a clean slate." Tyrone Holly, an employee who attended one of the meetings, similarly testified that Appold discussed bargaining in the following manner: "[Appold said] [t]hat it's a give and take situation. That he ain't going to just give something and just give it away. Like he said that we got the turkeys, the ham, and our cookie box, and if the union comes in there, a lot of that stuff we won't even have because they put it all on the table. And he said that we won't get probably none of that after it's all over with." In addition, Holly testified that Appold showed pictures of vandalism at the facility and stated that union people had committed these acts of vandalism.

The decision upheld findings of unfair labor practices in *Consolidated Biscuit Company* 346 NLRB 1175 (2006), which can be found at http://www.nlrb.gov/shared_files/Board%20Decisions/346/346101.pdf.

Source: *National Labor Relations Board v. Consolidated Biscuit Company*, 6th District Court of Appeals, slip op., Nov. 14, 2008; http://www.ca6.uscourts.gov/opinions.pdf/08a0697n-06.pdf.

out of unions. Campaigns against the EFCA have used stereotypes of mobster-like "labor bosses" to suggest union organizers are the heavies to worry about. On the Web site of the industry-supported Coalition for a Democratic Workplace

With "Protections" Like These . . .

In a choice often attributed to prejudice, Congress left several categories of working people out of the NLRA in 1935. The biggest excluded job categories were agricultural and domestic workers—jobs then held in large part by African Americans and women.

Ironically, the United Farm Workers (UFW) may have managed to organize California farm workers in the 1960s and 1970s because, as farm workers, its members were neither protected nor limited by the NLRA. The Taft-Hartley Act, which is part of the NLRA, did not apply to the UFW. Consequently, the Taft-Hartley secondary boycott laws could not prevent the UFW from organizing its boycott of California table grapes, which pressured grocery chains not to sell grapes from nonunion growers. Any union can ask the general public to stop buying a product, but the UFW could also conduct secondary picketing at grocery stores.

Taft-Hartley did limit how far other unions helped the UFW. The AFL-CIO supported the boycott for a while but withdrew after chain groceries threatened a lawsuit on secondary-boycott grounds. UFW leader Cesar Chavez told an interviewer:

> Since Taft-Hartley … labor solidarity just doesn't exist any more in the United States. Other unions can help out indirectly, but the Longshoremen are about the only ones that quit when they see a picket sign. Not the leadership but the membership—the men. In San Francisco, if you carry a picket sign anywhere near the docks, everything stops. It's sort of a tradition with them: the membership will not work behind picket lines. It's a small union, and they couldn't help us with money, but back in '65 they stopped the grapes at the docks twice in one week and got sued for eighty-five or ninety-five thousand dollars.*

*Peter Matthiesen, *Sal Si Puedes: Cesar Chavez and the New American Revolution*. New York: Random House, 1969, p. 152–153.

(MyPrivateBallot.com) in early 2009, visitors were greeted by a heavy-faced, glaring man in a suit who said threateningly, "Hey, you don't hafta be here. Take a walk."[11]

More than the EFCA is needed.

Neither "card check" nor the revised EFCA by itself can end restrictions on organizing. For example, they would not be able to overturn the ban on secondary tactics such as picketing companies that hire nonunion contractors. As it is, a big company can partly insulate itself against unions by hiring staff indirectly, through several different small-time nonunion contractors.

It remains to be seen if Congress will ban the "captive audience" meeting. As we saw with the Consolidated Biscuit example, employers can force employees to listen to antiunion speeches. Overly specific threats, like some made in the Consolidated Biscuit case, are prohibited. However, a carefully phrased presentation can scare people without crossing the officially recognized line. One study found that, in a sample of more than 400 NLRB-supervised union elections held during 1998 and 1999, 92 percent of employers held captive-audience meetings in which "more than half of all employers made threats to close all or part of the plant."[12]

The *Wall Street Journal* reported that Wal-Mart held captive-audience meetings for its managers in summer 2008 to discuss how unionization would be bad for the company. At the same meetings, the paper said, they discussed Barack Obama's support for unionization and the Employee Free Choice Act, which implied, though did not state, that the company wanted its employees to vote against Obama.[13]

Although Congress has done little to change the law of union organizing since Landrum-Griffin in 1959, the courts and the National Labor Relations Board have built up precedents favoring employers. The following are only two of the many examples.

First, the Supreme Court's *National Labor Relations Board v. Mackay Radio & Telegraph Co.* decision has thwarted unions since 1938. It allows employers to hire permanent replacement workers during a strike and to keep them after the strike is settled, even at the expense of strikers' jobs. The Landrum-Griffin Act and later court decisions have further protected both permanent replacements and workers who give up a strike early to ask for their jobs back.[14]

Second, the "Steelworkers Trilogy," a group of Supreme Court cases decided the same day in 1960, shut courts out of disputes involving union contracts that are sent to arbitration. Arbitration resembles a trial but is less formal; a privately hired arbitrator sits in place of a judge. The court found that once an arbitrator has issued a decision, courts cannot decide whether the decision was fair, only whether the arbitrator had power under the contract to make the decision. These three cases helped push labor law into a world of special administrative processes where procedure could be as important as justice.[15]

Tom Geoghegan writes bitterly that the liberal Supreme Court of the 1960s revived the antilabor injunction:

> In 1969, in the *Boys Markets* case, the Supreme Court held that it would now issue injunctions to enforce no-strike clauses in contracts. Then the Court went even further. It said it would "imply" no-strike clauses even if they weren't there, and it would enjoin all strikes over issues that were "arbitrable"—i.e., that could be raised before a neutral arbitrator.

Most strikes became illegal at union workplaces except when a contract came up for renewal. Geoghegan writes that in the 1970s, unofficial groups of coal miners, angry about pay and safety issues, staged unauthorized "wildcat" strikes while the union itself had to tamely follow the law.[16]

The laws put in place to prevent employers' unfair practices do not necessarily work. Complaints of illegal firings for union activity rose from the 1950s through the 1980s, until one in three federally supervised union elections saw illegal firings.[17] During this same period, employers developed a rich repertoire of antiunion tactics, including treating workers as temporary, defining them as "independent contractors," or hiring both union and nonunion contractors to undermine a union contract.

Union advocates particularly criticized the decision in the U.S. Supreme Court case of *Hoffman Plastic Compounds v. Labor Relations Board*.[18] In it, the court found that an undocumented immigrant who was fired illegally for union activity was not entitled to the usual repayment of back wages because he lacked a right to work in the United States. A Human Rights Watch report called the *Hoffman* decision a human rights violation.[19] Following this case, California passed a law extending state labor protections regardless of immigration status, but the national situation remains the same.[20]

In the last years of George W. Bush's administration, the National Labor Relations Board issued what many union supporters called antiunion decisions. Three cases in 2006, known as the "Kentucky River" opinions, expanded the definition of a "supervisor," potentially excluding millions of people from union membership. An AFL-CIO writer said it "essentially enables employers to make a supervisor out of any worker who has the authority to assign or direct another and uses independent judgment."[21]

Union members particularly complained of the "September Massacre," a group of 61 decisions issued in September 2007. These included the *Dana Corp.* decision, which, as the *Washington Post* put it, "required the auto-parts maker to post information on how workers could begin the process of decertifying a newly organized union, even though the company didn't oppose the organizing drive."[22]

Right-to-work or right to employer harassment?

As if the federal laws did not cause enough trouble for unions, state right-to-work laws make it more difficult to organize and defend them. Taft-Hartley long ago ended the "closed shop," a union contract that required employers to hire only union members. It does allow "union security agreements," which let the employer hire anyone but require each new employee to pay union dues or join the union.

Many states in the South, the Plains, and the inland West have gone beyond Taft-Hartley to prohibit union security agreements. These states' right-to-work laws typically make it illegal to require union membership or dues payments as a condition of employment. Such laws mean any employee can reject the union at any time, so an employer has reason to campaign against it all the time, not just during elections or contract negotiations.

Right-to-work laws developed in 1955, when a group of manufacturing employers founded the National Right to Work Committee, which promotes the "right to work" in language that imitates civil rights rhetoric. The committeee began by trying to break African-American civil rights alliance with unions by discussing the problem of union racism.[23] The Rev. Martin Luther King Jr. opposed right-to-work laws because he believed that segregationists supported them. He also noted, "Wherever these laws have been passed, wages are lower, job opportunities are fewer and there are no civil rights."[24]

Labor laws that affect nonunion workers need improvement.

During the last generation or two, employment laws enforceable by government regulators or private lawsuits have allowed individual employees, unionized or not, to assert rights through regulators like the Equal Employment Opportunity Commission (EEOC) and, if necessary, the courts. It was not always so. From 1905 to 1937, the U.S. Supreme Court struck down protective

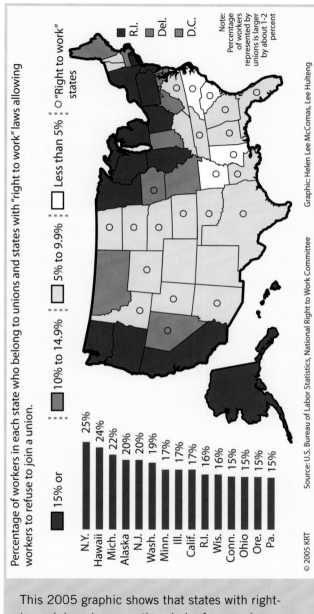

Percentage of workers in each state who belong to unions and states with "right to work" laws allowing workers to refuse to join a union.

Legend:
- ■ 15% or
- ▨ 10% to 14.9%
- ▨ 5% to 9.9%
- □ Less than 5%
- ○ "Right to work" states

- ■ R.I.
- ■ Del.
- ■ D.C.

Note: Percentage of workers represented by unions is larger by about 1-2 percent

State	Percentage
N.Y.	25%
Hawaii	24%
Mich.	22%
Alaska	20%
N.J.	20%
Wash.	19%
Minn.	17%
Ill.	17%
Calif.	17%
R.I.	16%
Wis.	16%
Conn.	15%
Ohio	15%
Ore.	15%
Pa.	15%

© 2005 KRT

Source: U.S. Bureau of Labor Statistics, National Right to Work Committee

Graphic: Helen Lee McComas, Lee Hulteng

This 2005 graphic shows that states with right-to-work laws have, on the whole, fewer union members than states that do not have such laws.

legislation on working hours and conditions as unconstitutional. In 1937, under pressure from the administration of Franklin D. Roosevelt, the court finally endorsed wage and hour laws in the same reversal that upheld the NLRA,[25] which protects some people who are not union members if two or more employees present a complaint or request to an employer through "concerted activity," or if one speaks to the employer on behalf of others. An individual who complains alone is not protected even if the complaint might help coworkers.[26]

Our civil rights laws, going back to statutes enacted after the Civil War, are among the great achievements in workers' rights. In the last generation or so, unions have helped to pass such laws. Modern civil rights laws began with the Civil Rights Act of 1964. Its Title VII created the EEOC, strengthening individual employees' rights to seek protection from regulators or courts.[27] There followed the 1967 Age Discrimination in Employment Act;[28] the 1970 Occupational Safety and Health Act;[29] the 1973 Rehabilitation Act, which created early disability rights protections;[30] the 1974 Employee Retirement Income Security Act (ERISA), which provides limited protections for pensions and health care;[31] the 1990 Americans with Disabilities Act on disability civil rights;[32] and the 1993 Family and Medical Leave Act, which provides limited protections for employees who take time off for illness, childbirth, or family caretaking.[33]

Many of these laws grant employees their own "private right of action." That is, if a regulatory agency will not help, an aggrieved employee can take the employer to court directly. Legislative and court system changes in the 1970s encouraged such lawsuits by allowing more discrimination plaintiffs to collect attorneys' fees if they won cases. This meant lawyers could hope to be well paid to represent low-income clients.[34]

Sometimes civil rights laws fail to provide the appropriate remedy against injustice, as in the case of *Lilly Ledbetter v. Goodyear Tire & Rubber Co., Inc.* Lilly Ledbetter, a supervisor with Goodyear for almost 20 years, learned just before her retirement that she had been underpaid for most of her career compared with men who did the same work. She filed an EEOC complaint, then a lawsuit. Although the jury found that Goodyear did discriminate against Ledbetter, a Supreme Court majority decided Ledbetter had no right to compensation for any unfair decision made more than 180 days before she filed the complaint. Because the company had committed no new injustices during those last 180 days, the court found Ledbetter had no grounds to sue.[35] One of President Barack Obama's first acts in office was to sign a newly passed federal law that removed the 180-day requirement.

Several other kinds of employment law affect workers' freedoms and futures. Among the oldest is the nationwide system of state workers' compensation laws, which reflect an awkward compromise reached around 1910 to bring workers or their families at least some payment for workplace injuries or deaths. This compromise ended legal principles that had protected employers against liability, including the "fellow-servant rule," which held that it was not the employer's fault if a fellow employee's carelessness caused an injury; the concept of "contributory negligence," which blamed any victim whose own mistake helped cause the injury; and the "assumption of risk" doctrine, which held employees could not complain of injuries in a job they already knew was dangerous. Workers' compensation makes fixed payments to people with work-related injuries or illnesses. At first it only paid for injuries from sudden accidents. Later, occupational disease qualified as well.[36] The payments tend to be less than people can get in normal personal injury lawsuits over accidental injuries suffered on their own time.

Other laws on workers' income rights offer lukewarm protection at best. Employers are not required to provide pensions and health care coverage and these benefits are only minimally protected once promised. Tom Geoghegan recently wrote, "I'd say that with a competent lawyer, any employer can cancel any promise to any worker."[37]

Current Labor Laws Are Unfair to Employers

Pro-union language treats Taft-Hartley and Landrum-Griffin as antiunion laws that unfairly restrict the right to organize. However, they were passed for good reason: corruption within the Teamsters and other unions. One example on legislators' minds was the Detroit Teamsters' 1946 use of secondary boycott threats to shake down small, often family-run, grocery stores. The Teamsters tried to make the stores pay five dollars apiece for "associate membership" permits, plus monthly "union dues," before they could receive their food orders through Teamster-organized wholesalers. Russell writes:

> Hoffa scoffed at the suggestion that his union depended on violence to force the grocers to sign. "That's ridiculous," he sneered. "There is no need for violence of any sort. Our packinghouse dockworkers will simply refuse

60

to serve them and the truckers will not deliver to their places of business. They'll have to join." To help enforce the boycott, carloads of Teamster "permit salesmen" formed blockades around loading docks at packing-houses and produce terminals, physically sealing off the merchants from their supplies.[1]

Landrum-Griffin protects honest people on all sides.

The Landrum-Griffin Act passed in 1959, just after the Senate's McClellan Committee hearings on union corruption.[2] Provisions with the International Brotherhood of Teamsters in mind banned forms of secondary boycotts that had not been fully covered by Taft-Hartley, such as "hot cargo" contract clauses in contracts that required employers to refuse an antiunion employer's shipments. The act further restricted picketing and stopped most ways of organizing a union through external pressure rather than through direct appeals to prospective new members. It allowed more federal regulation of unions' internal affairs, under the new assumption that members needed protection against their own unions.

The Landrum-Griffin Act helps honest unions as well as honest employers. During the United Farm Workers' (UFW) organizing campaign of the 1960s, a rival union, the Agricultural Workers Freedom to Work Association, appeared with a friendlier attitude to growers. Although everyone suspected employers were behind it, it took a filing required by the Landrum-Griffin Act to reveal that the new group really was an illegal "company union," founded and supported primarily by growers and the rightwing John Birch Society.[3]

Labor laws protect workers, but not managers, against person-to-person pressure. For example, the decision in *NLRB v. Weingarten, Inc.* gave workers the right to have a union shop steward present during interviews that may result in discipline.[4]

Free choice or forced choice?

As the Obama administration began in 2009, lobbyists for businesses and employers were concentrating their efforts against the "card check" proposal that was then the main provision of the proposed Employee Free Choice Act by suggesting that it would put workers in danger by making it important for workers to sign union support cards openly, rather than vote by secret ballot. In other words, once union organizers found out who had not signed the cards, they might threaten or harass individual workers into signing.[5] The Associated Builders and Contractors (ABC) invited member employers to place flyers in workers' pay envelopes captioned, "Who Do You Want in the Voting Booth with You?"[6]

The Giant Inflatable Picketer

What's the difference between illegal "picketing" and free speech? And when is a giant inflatable rat a "picketer"?

These questions came up a few years ago in Florida when members of the Sheet Metal Workers' Union protested a decision by Brandon Regional Medical Center to use a nonunion contractor, Workers Temporary Staffing (WTS), for renovation work. Taft-Hartley forbids "secondary picketing" at a job site where the target employer works for someone else, so instead the union was handing out flyers (or "handbilling"), not patrolling with signs. But the union had also brought a giant inflatable rat, which they used to call nonunion WTS a "rat employer." A case summary said "The rat was twelve feet wide at the base, wore a sign that read 'Workers Temporary Staffing,' and sat 'upright, smiling, with a cigar in its mouth.' The hospital, Brandon Regional Medical Center, complained to the NLRB, saying the rat, though inanimate, was an illegal "picketer." An administrative law judge agreed.*

In 2009, however, the New Jersey Supreme Court overturned the conviction of union officer Wayne DeAngelo for violating a local ordinance of Lawrence Township against "balloon signs or other inflated signs (excepting grand opening signs) ... displayed for the purpose of attracting the attention of pedestrians and

Despite decades-long efforts to clean up their image, unions have not abandoned the use of threats. For example, the National Labor Relations Board's 1984 *Clear Pine Mouldings* case recounts:

> One week prior to the strike Sittser and two other employees "cornered" employee Johnny Webb against a wall at work and told Webb he would have to go on strike as voted by the other employees. When Webb said that he had been on vacation when the strike vote was taken, the employees began shoving Webb, and Sittser stated that Webb should watch out because they might burn his house or garage or something.[7]

motorists." DeAngelo's International Brotherhood of Electrical Workers, Local 269, had used an inflatable rat to protest a nonunion contractor at a Gold's Gym. The court upheld the rat on constitutional free speech grounds without mentioning labor law: "There is no evidence to suggest that a rat balloon is significantly more harmful to aesthetics or safety than a similar item being displayed as an advertisement or commercial logo used in a seven-day grand opening promotion. Nor is there any evidence to suggest that the ordinance 'is necessary to serve a compelling state interest and that it is narrowly drawn to achieve that end.'"**

Except, even if the giant rats are legal, are they a good idea when they provoke so much anger? In 2008, some upstate New York union leaders publicly cut up their rat balloons to symbolize their willingness to negotiate with employers.***

*Tzvi Mackson-Landsberg, "Is a Giant Inflatable Rat an Unlawful Secondary Picket Under Section 8(b)(4)(ii)(B) of the National Labor Relations Act?" *Cardozo Law Review*, vol. 28, pp. 1519–1561 (2006); http://www.lawmemo.com/articles/rat.pdf.

**State v. Wayne DeAngelo*, New Jersey Supreme Court, Feb. 5, 2009; http://lawlibrary.rutgers.edu/courts/supreme/a-73-07.opn.html.

***Kris Dunn, "Unions Go Upstream—Take Down the Inflatable Rat Used in Picketing," November 24, 2008; http://www.hrcapitalist.com/2008/11/unions-go-upstream--deflate-inflatable-rat-used-in-picketing.html.

Just recently, the NLRB found that leaders of a Teamsters bus drivers' local had threatened a dissident member; he accused them of breaking his windshield, and the union president said that if he "had a beef" with the dissident, he would "break something else."[8]

The *Dana Corp.* decision, criticized by union advocates as among the worst of the "September Massacre" cases, provides a preview of the way "card check" might work. The NLRB had its reasons to wonder if this particular "card check" really expressed potential members' wishes. Here, the union and two employers agreed that the employers would remain neutral during the union's organizing campaign and each would voluntarily recognize the union as its employees' representative if a majority signed support cards. The union turned in enough cards for recognition, but then some employees in each bargaining unit petitioned to have the union "decertified," to end union recognition before it began. The board ordered each employer to post a notice explaining employees' rights to a decertification election. Its decision noted people might have signed union support cards for reasons such as fear of offending a coworker or because of misinformation about the card's legal significance.[9]

Conservative columnist Stefan Gleason claimed that employees had been "individually browbeaten" into signing cards for the Dana Corp. union by organizers who got their home addresses. The board decision said the company "asserted that the authorization cards were coercively obtained or otherwise tainted," but it presented no evidence.[10]

Is the NLRB partial to employers?

Pro-union advocates usually say the NLRB does too much for employers. Antiunion advocates disagree. Just before the "September Massacre" of 2007, Gleason wrote that President George W. Bush's NLRB "has failed to correct literally dozens of activist rulings handed down by President Clinton's NLRB." Bush was slow to appoint members to the NLRB. Those he did choose were not people the Senate would confirm, so they served short "recess appointment" terms or none at all. Gleason noted that Bush "didn't even install a Republican majority until nearly a year into his presidency." If you add up various gaps, the NLRB was missing at least one of its five members during more than three years of the eight-year Bush administration. When President Obama took office the board had only two serving members: Clinton-appointed Democrat Wilma Liebman and Bush-appointed Republican Peter Schaumber.[11]

The Taft-Hartley Act does more than just restrain unions. It also requires employers to tolerate some aspects of union organizing drives within workplaces and prohibits them from firing or discriminating against known pro-union employees. The NLRB punishes violations of these rules.

In 2007, Republican NLRB chairman Robert Battista, then about to end his term, said that "of the majority of unfair labor practice decisions issued in September, the board found one or more violations of the act by the employer involved." He added:

> During my 5-year tenure as chairman, the NLRB recovered a total of $604 million in back pay with 13,279 employees offered reinstatement. In fiscal 2007, the NLRB held 1,559 representation elections in under 2 months. The unions won over half of them. Over the same period, two-thirds of the 22,000 unfair labor practice charges that the NLRB received were investigated and resolved within 4 months. Of charges found to have merit, some 90 percent are settled prior to the issuance of a complaint.[12]

A right-to-work is exactly that.

The Taft-Hartley Act's Subsection 158(a)(3) allows employers to enter "union security" agreements, which can require every newly hired worker, pro-union or not, to join the union or sometimes to pay union dues. Unions may demand and get "union security" clauses as part of contract agreements, unless a state right-to-work law protects both the employer and anti-union employees, by prohibiting these agreements within the state. Right-to-work laws protect employees' rights to keep their jobs without joining a union or paying its dues. The National Right to Work Legal Defense Foundation (NRWLDF) counts 22 states with right-to-work laws.

The NRWLDF has repeatedly challenged how unions may spend dues paid by unwilling members. In *Locke v. Karass*, it represented Maine public employees who did not belong to the Maine State Employees Association but still had to pay it a service fee under a union security agreement. The NRWLDF found it unfair that the Maine union sent some of the security fee money to its parent, the Service Employees International Union (SEIU), which used it for pro-union legal expenses. The U.S. Supreme Court upheld this use of service fees in Locke although it had previously ruled in *Davenport v. Washington Education Association* that when public employees who do not belong to a union have to pay fees, states may require unions to get the payers' specific permission before the money can go to political spending.[13] In *Ysursa v. Pocatello Education Association*, the court ruled that an Idaho state law could allow payroll deductions for union dues while it prohibited payroll deductions for union political purposes.[14]

Antiunion groups would like to make all states right-to-work. The National Right to Work Act has been repeatedly introduced in Congress, most recently in 2007. In that year, it attracted 71 cosponsors in the 435-member House of Representatives but did not pass.[15]

Labor laws overburden nonunion employers too.

Some labor laws apply to large corporations only, but many apply to small business owners who cannot afford lawyers or human resource specialists. While small business advocates may not necessarily be against things like civil rights, pregnancy leave, or fair pay, federal laws sometimes make little sense in a particular small business context.[16]

Many of the most expensive federal laws for business owners have to do with social services: employee benefits and pensions, contributions to insurance funds for workers' compensation, unemployment, and Social Security. Under the Family and

Poster Requirements

In all U.S. businesses that employ anyone beyond the owner, you will find a wall, bulletin board, or office door covered with technical-looking posters. These are notices required by law that each employer must display to inform employees of their rights and duties—mostly rights. Poster requirements differ by state and also vary by the kind of work done, number of people employed, and whether the employer has government contracts. Subjects may include minimum wages, overtime pay, equal employment opportunity, smoking rules, workers' compensation rights, paydays, safety rules, pregnancy leave, and many others.

State and federal agencies that require posters usually provide them online for free download. These are just samples of the sites:

U.S. Department of Labor:
http://www.dol.gov/osbp/sbrefa/poster/matrix.htm

Texas Workforce Commission:
http://www.twc.state.tx.us/ui/lablaw/posters.html

California Department of Industrial Relations:
http://www.dir.ca.gov/wpnodb.html

New York State Department of Labor:
http://www.labor.state.ny.us/workerprotection/laborstandards/employer/posters.shtm

Because not all small businesses know which posters are required, an industry has developed to sell the required displays. As of early 2009, a company called GovDocs (at http://www.laborlawposter.com/site/index.html) was charging $79 for a plastic-covered sheet with the standard posters for a specific state, or $29 for the right to download the same posters from GovDocs.

Medical Leave Act, employers must give workers time off for their own pregnancy or illness, to take care of a newborn or newly adopted child, or to take care of a family member who is ill, without replacing them permanently.[17] Some argue that liberals have tried to make business owners fill roles that, in Europe, are played by social-democratic government programs. For example, instead of publicly provided national health care, the United States has employee health-care coverage regulations for businesses, supplemented by personal injury lawsuits, which are often filed to recover medical bills. (To get a sense of the costs and paperwork that a small business faces for each employee, see the Internal Revenue Service's "Employment Taxes" rule summary page, currently located at http://www.irs.gov/businesses/small/article/0,,id=172179,00.html.)

Employers must also deal with the consequences of anti-discrimination laws, under which managers sometimes get into trouble even when they try to be fair. Misunderstandings can lead people to accuse each other of prejudice. Or employees who have done something wrong or badly at work may use discrimination charges to avoid what are actually reasonable consequences for their actions.

Newer legal definitions of discrimination may be misunderstood. For example, when the Americans with Disabilities Act took effect in the 1990s, some people thought "disability accommodations" referred only to physical things like wheelchair ramps. In fact they can include flexible management decisions, such as an agreement to let an employee start work late because he or she suffers side effects from medication in the morning.[18]

"Affirmative action," meaning policies that take race, ethnicity, gender, and age into consideration in an attempt to promote equal opportunity, have split both unions and employers.[19] Affirmative action is supposed to go beyond the mere absence of discrimination and make up for past wrongs. The general principle is that when two people are equally qualified for a job or other opportunity, the member of a group that has suffered discrimination should be chosen. Sometimes numerical affirmative action hiring goals are set. For example, since 1980 the Department of Labor's Office of Federal Contract Compliance Programs has required that federal construction contractors should try to make sure that at least 6.9 percent of their employees are women.[20] Court affirmative action orders setting minimum minority membership percentages integrated some racially discriminatory labor unions in the 1970s.[21]

Although private employers may voluntarily adopt affirmative action principles, the courts may require them to use affirmative action to make up for past discrimination. The general law for private employers is "equal employment opportunity," which merely prohibits discrimination. Employers with more than 100 employees must file annual reports showing the percentages of employees in certain types of work who are women or belong to federally defined minority groups.[22]

Under "prevailing wage" laws, especially the Davis-Bacon and Related Acts' federal contract requirements, government contractors must pay what is officially recognized as the usual pay rate, including benefits, in the designated place, for the designated type of work.[23] The laws can result in high pay for relatively unskilled workers and can harm poor people by making public service projects such as affordable housing more expensive. A number of writers argue that the Davis-Bacon requirements are bad for the economy.[24] The very detailed Davis-Bacon wage determinations site (http://www.gpo.gov/davisbacon/pubweek.html) shows the degree of bureaucracy involved.

It is hard to maintain that the majority of employers are against workplace safety, but sometimes safety rules are unfairly enforced. For example, the U.S. General Accounting Office (now the General Accountability Office) reported in 2000: "Establishments experiencing labor unrest are about 6.5 times more likely to be inspected by OSHA than establishments not experiencing labor unrest (8.6 percent inspected compared with about 1.3 percent) during fiscal years 1994 through 1998."[25]

Arguably, employers should not be made to substitute for government officials. It is unfair to saddle employers with extra responsibilities because the United States has no national health-care system and benefits for unemployed people are low. On the immigration issue, employers should not have to serve as immigration inspectors, nor be penalized for failing to invade their employees' privacy. In fact, many employers have been on the side of illegal immigrants while native-born workers have conducted often racially biased campaigns against them.[26] It is not wrong for employers to welcome immigrants who want to work hard and possess useful skills.

Summary

Labor laws that restrict union organizing tactics were passed because of real union bullying. The proposed "card check" legislation and the Employee Free Choice Act measure before Congress could open up new avenues for union coercion by removing secret ballot protections from the union recognition process. The National Labor Relations Board and the courts have been accused of being too tough on unions, but some anti-union advocates disagree. Right-to-work laws protect employees against having to join unions they don't support. Many labor laws affect nonunion employers by imposing paperwork and other requirements. While liberals may have tried over the years to impose public social support duties on individual business owners, it is clear that such requirements can be especially tough on small businesses.

Unions Give Working People a Fairer Deal

From a pro-union point of view, unions promote fairness in workplaces, industries, and societies. Unions do sometimes use their strength in numbers to act on the basis of prejudices or claim unfair privileges. Still, wages and working conditions would be worse if employees could not make themselves heard through unions.

Richard Freeman and James Medoff have described unions as having two "faces": a "monopoly" face and a "collective voice" face. The "collective voice" face is unions' constructive side, which humanizes working conditions, stands up to mistreatment, and asserts workers' right to participate in "industrial democracy." They note this side of unions improves fairness and business efficiency by helping employees to propose improvements and forcing managers to justify their actions. For example, managers cannot impose pay differences based on favoritism or work rules based on personal whims. Unions defend older workers, who often cannot afford to leave their current jobs, whereas non-union employers may cater to younger workers, who generally can more easily find jobs elsewhere if they are unhappy.

Unions' "monopoly" face is the side that uses strength in numbers to enforce demands. This is the side of unions that people accuse of helping some workers at the expense of others. The term "monopoly" recognizes that unions, like businesses, get power by asserting control over a product. When businesses control a commodity like oil, they can choke off its supply to force up prices. Union members can do the same with what they have to sell, which is their labor.

The "monopoly" face can produce unfairness; for example, unions have the power to obtain higher wages for union members who do the same work as nonunion workers, perhaps under pleasanter conditions and more slowly. Some nonunion workers may not get jobs at all. However, unions can improve wages and working conditions for whole industries. In fact, nonunion employers are more likely to treat people fairly if they fear the possibility of unionization.

The "monopoly" face is what antiunion campaigners have in mind when they accuse unions of harming the economy. Freeman and Medoff maintain, however, that most unions can only negotiate for wage increases, not dictate them, and wage increases are not unions' only goals. Unions might also, for example, give up a pay raise to protect more members' jobs. They say unions cannot raise wages significantly except in rare cases: if they control a whole market, or if they organize in companies that do not compete directly with other firms to lower labor costs.[1]

A monopoly of skilled labor is relatively easy to achieve under certain circumstances; it is possible to organize all the air traffic controllers, pro ballplayers, or senior-level nurses because they are so few in number. Unions with low-skilled members cannot establish monopoly power as they are easily undercut by low-wage outsiders in a "race to the bottom." These differences have led to separate styles of organizing, historically known as "craft" and "industrial" organizing.

Craft unionism is the senior and more cautious kind, associated with the old American Federation of Labor (the AFL, as in AFL-CIO). Craft unions bring together relatively small groups of workers who practice the same skilled "craft." Industrial unionism, associated with the Congress of Industrial Organizations (CIO), developed for semiskilled workers in large factories. It succeeded best in industries such as steel, mining, and auto manufacturing.

Unions can be inclusive.

Either kind of union can behave well toward outsiders. Craft unions can train outsiders to do their kind of work. Industrial unions can welcome them as members and invite them to join labor actions like strikes. Unfortunately, unions do face powerful temptations to treat outsiders badly, to try to get rid of them, because an individual union member benefits most when qualified workers are in short supply and therefore highly paid. Each new union member is an equally advantaged competitor. At their best, unions rise above this temptation.

Most labor conflicts have at least three sides: union members and supporters, management, and actual or potential "scabs," meaning the outsiders willing to do union members' jobs for less. Traditional union culture demonizes "scabs" and accuses them of wanting to hurt fellow workers. But these replacement workers just want a job and may be unaware that they are replacing or undercutting union members.

As the writer Jack London had already noticed in 1904, "Such is the tangle of conflicting interests in a tooth-and-nail society that people cannot avoid being scabs, are often made so against their desires, and unconsciously."[2] On the other hand, a nastier, more widely quoted definition of scab workers is also attributed to London: "A scab is a two-legged animal with a

(continues on page 76)

The PATCO Strike: Hang Together or Separately

The 1981 destruction of the Professional Air Traffic Controllers Organization (PATCO) began a devastating joint attack against unions by government and business during the Reagan administration. It happened in part because different kinds of unions failed to stick together, and all unions suffered for it.

PATCO was a classic craft union. Until 1981, it represented most of the nation's air traffic controllers. It is hard to think of any place where high professional standards and job satisfaction could be more necessary than in an airport control tower, where calm, steady figures have to guide pilots past each other through crowded airspace. An air controller's missed move could mean hundreds dead. Craft unions tend to be conservative; PATCO was exceptionally so. In 1980, PATCO had endorsed Ronald Reagan, the Republican candidate for president.

In the 1970s, PATCO was in running disputes over pay, hours, and conditions with the controllers' employer, the Federal Aviation Administration (FAA). The controllers were tired of authoritarian ex-military supervisors, dangerously aging equipment, and staffing cuts that could leave too few controllers guiding too many planes. They wanted a 32-hour workweek and relief from high-paid but exhausting hours of mandatory overtime. Some controllers said stress was harming their health.

PATCO went on strike in 1981. In response, Reagan fired 11,345 controllers for staging an illegal strike. Reagan's administration then arranged for the union to be decertified, stripped of its status as bargaining representative. These were shocking acts at the time, but union and liberal support for PATCO was lukewarm. From a pro-union point of view, it was a failure of solidarity. Because employers and the public saw that a powerful union could be broken, additional union busting followed. PATCO had broken ranks with other unions to support Reagan, but other unions should not have abandoned PATCO.

(continues on page 76)

(opposite page) Nearly a thousand supporters for the Professional Air Traffic Controllers Organization (PATCO) gather on City Hall Plaza in Boston, Massachusetts, to show support for the striking controllers on August 24, 1981. Speakers from various labor parties spoke against the Reagan administration's tactics in dealing with the strike.

(continued from page 74)

PATCO's destruction did worsen air traffic control. Staff cuts at control towers ranged from 7 percent to 57 percent, in part because not enough replacements could be found. Chicago's staff of controllers fell from 337 to 169 between mid-1981 and mid-1987. In 1985, a General Accounting Office (GAO) survey found controllers and their supervisors "thought they were being stretched too thin," and a consultant said air traffic was less safe than before the strike.

Sources: Rebecca Pels, "The Pressures of PATCO: Strikes and Stress in the 1980s," *Essays in History*, vol. 37, 1995, Corcoran Department of History, University of Virginia; http://etext. virginia.edu/journals/EH/EH37/Pels.html; "Labor's Coolness Toward Controllers," *Boston Globe*, August 13, 1981, p. 1; GAO, "FAA Staffing: Air Traffic Controllers' Work Load and Operational Performance: Fact Sheet for the Chairman, Subcommittee on Transportation and Related Agencies, Committee on Appropriations, United States Senate," Rept. No. GAO/RCED-87-138FS, May 1987; http://archive.gao.gov/d2t4/132903.pdf; Herbert R. McLure, GAO, Testimony, "FAA Work Force Issues" before Senate Appropriations Subcommittee on Transportation, May 7, 1987; http://archive.gao.gov/d39t12/132875.pdf.

(continued from page 73)

corkscrew soul, a water brain, a combination backbone of jelly and glue. Where others have hearts, he carries a tumor of rotten principles."[3] While it is true that some unions have treated scabs badly, to the point of physical injury and worse, they learned in the old CIO days, and are learning again, that inclusiveness is the best way for embattled unions, especially those representing low-skilled, low-paid workers, to gain membership and power.

There have always been unions that organized very poor people. Parts of the labor movement continue to preserve Eugene Debs's austere sense of mission: "[W]hile there is a lower class, I am in it; while there is a criminal element, I am of it; while there is a soul in prison, I am not free."[4]

Until the early 1930s on the West Coast, and for even longer on the East Coast, respectable union members looked down on the longshoremen who loaded and unloaded ship cargoes piece by piece in the days before container shipping. The work was handed out piecemeal in a way that kept all but a favored few unemployed much of the time.[5] In most ports, the "wharf rats" got jobs through the "shape-up," much as day laborers do now: Every morning workers stand in a crowd and wait to be hired for a day or part of a day, or not at all. Sometimes longshoremen had to beg or bribe the hiring bosses for work, or choose between a 24-hour shift or nothing. On the West Coast, unions had brief successes at the start of the twentieth century, but from about World War I until 1933 the employers ran waterfront hiring, either through employer-dominated hiring halls, as in Seattle, or through employer-dominated unions such as San Francisco's "blue book" system. The fierce 1934 general strike by West Coast longshoremen made employers abolish the "shape-up." The union replaced it with indoor hiring halls that tried to eliminate favoritism by distributing jobs in an impartial rotation.[6]

Unfortunately, union corruption is part of this story. The West Coast longshoremen's union began as part of the International Longshoremen's Association (ILA), but quickly broke with ILA leaders and became the more leftwing International Longshoremen's and Warehousemen's Union (ILWU, now the International Longshore and Warehouse Union). The ILA on the East Coast became known for associations with organized crime. It continued to support the shape-up until 1953, when state authorities and the national AFL forced the issue. ILA officers would cooperate with employers to pick "hiring bosses" who chose the union officers' favorites for jobs, while keeping other waterfront job seekers intimidated and grateful for whatever work they could get. This kind of shape-up favoritism is portrayed in the film *On the Waterfront*.[7] Scholar Howard Kimeldorf notes, "By the early 1950s . . . both longshore unions had been expelled from their respective labor federations: the ILWU for following the Communist Party; the ILA for collaborating with the shipowners."[8] Today, both unions are still around (see http://www.

ilaunion.org and http://www.ilwu.org), but their power has diminished since the 1960s, when shipping containers reduced the number of workers needed in ports.[9]

The United Farm Workers (UFW) also brought together people with the hard-to-organize characteristics of extreme poverty and unstable employment. In the 1960s and 1970s, the UFW even organized migrant workers, who many felt could not be organized because they traveled much of the year.[10] The Association of Community Organizations for Reform Now (ACORN) organized unions in low-paid, often short-term jobs like fast food, hotel, and home care work. In 1984, the ACORN unions merged into the more established Service Employees International Union (SEIU), and changed it from inside. The SEIU has since done some of the nation's most creative organizing among low-wage workers.[11]

The SEIU's Justice for Janitors campaign has been especially successful. Begun in 1986 and expanded in the 1990s, the campaign organizes janitors who clean large buildings.[12] Often the cleaners' direct employers are small firms, but the offices they clean have reputations to lose. Justice for Janitors uses tactics such as sit-ins and protest marches to shame the buildings' owners. (The campaign has faced some charges of illegal "secondary" tactics. Generally the union avoids Taft-Hartley restrictions by holding protests away from work sites, where they are considered protected free speech under the First Amendment.[13]) In 2006, 400 low-paid janitors at the University of Miami won a contract through a Justice for Janitors campaign that involved the academic community in protests including a hunger strike. Most recently, SEIU was using similar methods to organize security guards.[14]

Union members and campus activists are finding they have much in common—a considerable change from 1970, when a group of construction workers clashed with student anti-war demonstrators in New York City.[15] College students have organized efforts such as United Students Against Sweatshops, which among other things tries to ensure that universities' logo-marked clothing is made for a fair wage.[16]

Some other surprising alliances have developed. During the 1999 Seattle demonstrations against the World Trade Organization talks, members of industrial unions marched alongside environmental activists, including some in sea turtle costumes. One sign read, "Turtles and Teamsters, Together at Last."[17]

Other efforts outside mainstream unions involve day labor centers, or hiring halls, for immigrant day laborers. Pay is often higher through the centers, and a day's work no longer begins with a risky leap into a stranger's truck. Nonetheless, many day laborers are undocumented immigrants reluctant to assert their rights for fear someone will call immigration authorities.[18]

Union members are not unjustly rich.

A common criticism is that unions spend too much time helping people who already make good wages—the $30-per-hour auto assembly workers rather than $7-per-hour farm workers. Unions are not charities. They are organizations formed by people who prefer *not* to be poor. Besides that, high-paid assembly workers are not typical union members. The UFW and Justice for Janitors members are in there too. The union wage was $886 per week in 2008, or $46,072 per year on average, meaning many union members earn less. By comparison, the U.S. median family income for fiscal 2008 was $61,500. It takes more than one average union wage just to bring a household income to this level.[19]

Moreover, it is difficult to organize very poor people. Poverty is so full of risk that those living in it tend to protect themselves psychologically by not thinking about the future. Often, poor people are afraid of attracting powerful people's attention. Leaders on all sides of the U.S. union tradition have feared that very poor members may be irresponsible or unreasonable.

Even Karl Marx opposed organizing the "lumpenproletariat," or "ragged poor."[20]

It's unfair to recycle old corruption charges.

Antiunion campaigners sound dated when they repeat "Big Labor" and "union boss" in every press release. In fact, reform movements have changed the core of the labor movement. The notorious Teamsters moved toward reform in 1991 with the election of outsider candidate Ron Carey as president. Later Carey was disgraced by corruption charges of his own, and the union returned to old-school loyalties by electing James P. Hoffa, son of Jimmy Hoffa, as Carey's successor. A change had begun, one that the hard-hitting group Teamsters for a Democratic Union continues to press. In 1995, reform candidate John Sweeney became president of the AFL-CIO. In 2005, the Change to Win coalition of unions left the AFL-CIO, calling for more organizing and more political distance from the Democratic Party. The Change to Win alliance included the Teamsters, the SEIU, and the UNITE-HERE textile, laundry, hotel, and restaurant workers coalition. The continuing union movement shake-up has since produced more reforms, rebellions, and alliances that were still in flux as of mid-2009. That said, it is clear labor is reaching out to the underdogs again. For example, the labor movement's newest recruits, like Justice for Janitors' SEIU members, need unions to protect their basic rights.

Unions protect everyone's rights.

Unions have advanced many kinds of civil rights. The African-American civil rights movement owes much to the Brotherhood of Sleeping Car Porters. Founded in 1925 under A. Philip Randolph, its first president, this union brought together the all-black service staff of the Pullman Company's overnight passenger rail cars, known as the "Pullman porters." Wages and conditions won by the Brotherhood of Sleeping Car Porters from the 1930s on made it possible for many African-American families to reach the middle class and to claim fuller roles as citizens. The 1963 March on Washington, an essential event in the civil rights of black Americans, was organized in part by A. Philip Randolph.

The Rev. Martin Luther King Jr. believed in unions. When he was assassinated in Memphis in 1968, he was visiting that city to support a strike by African-American sanitation workers. History books often show pictures of the garbage truck drivers who marched with King on his last day of life, holding signs that answered demeaning work conditions with the words, "I Am a Man."[21]

Title VII of the Civil Rights Act of 1964 brought federal labor investigators to small Southern towns where descendants of slaves ordinarily had no outside protection against abuses. While it is true that Title VII also forced racist unions to integrate, that fact does not mean present-day unions are bad, just that Title VII changed the labor movement for the better. Over time, unions accepted civil rights language and ideas.[22] Nelson Lichtenstein writes, "Even in their shrunken state, trade unions are the most multiracial of all institutions and the most committed to the mobilization of those at the bottom of society."[23]

In the 1960s and 1970s, the women's rights movement used existing unions to campaign for equal rights, and also created unions of maids and welfare recipients. Additionally, a union-like Wages for Housework campaign formed. Unions slowly accepted their duty to combat workplace problems caused by gender discrimination. For example, airline stewardesses persuaded male union officers to oppose advertisements and uniform styles that suggested the female cabin crew were sexually available to male travelers.[24]

Immigrants, from the mid-1800s to the present, have advanced best when they formed their own unions or found majority-group union members who would work with them. It was true for the immigrants who founded the garment workers' unions in the 1800s, and it is true now for groups like the Chinese Staff and Workers' Association in New York City, which organized restaurant and sweatshop workers and pushed the old-school garment unions to pay attention to new immigrants in the late twentieth century.[25]

Employers have often kept their workforces divided by encouraging xenophobia, the fear or dislike of that which is unknown or different. Through the labor upheavals of the late nineteenth and early twentieth centuries, prejudice against foreigners was an important weapon in antiunion publicity. Around 1902, George F. Baer, president of the Philadelphia and Reading Coal and Iron Company, allegedly said Pennsylvania's hard-coal miners "don't suffer . . . why, they can't even speak English."[26]

Throughout California's agricultural history, employers often recruited disadvantaged people to serve as a low-paid labor force. When the new crop of workers got settled enough to assert rights and buy land, the growers labeled them as dangerous strangers, expelled them (sometimes violently), and brought in a new disadvantaged group. It happened to members of local Indian tribes, freed slaves after the Civil War, and immigrants from China, Japan, Armenia, the Philippines, and from Mexico and other parts of Latin America. The Dust Bowl migrants, primarily whites from southern and central states who lost farms during the Great Depression, fell into this pattern as well. The internment of people of Japanese descent, both immigrants and U.S. citizens, during World War II, which occurred after the Japanese bombing of the U.S. naval base at Pearl Harbor in December 1941, forced thousands of people to abandon their property or sell it cheaply when they entered government camps. It may be argued that the internment resulted in part the growers' backlash against members of an immigrant group who had become too successful.[27]

Summary

Unions at their best include and help nonmembers rather than treat them as competing scabs. Some unions have done well by organizing disadvantaged potential scabs, though it is difficult to organize very poor people. Not all union members are $30-an-hour autoworkers. The old corruption charges of the 1950s are getting dated. Over the past 20 years, mainstream unions have reformed and returned to grassroots organizing. Although they have sometimes used prejudice to their advantage, unions have also been important in civil rights movements. At their best, union activists understand that racism and other forms of discrimination only help employers.

Unions Help Some Working People at Others' Expense

J ust because an organization calls itself a labor union does not mean the people in it, particularly its leaders, are heroes fighting for the downtrodden. Unions are not necessarily kind to each other, let alone to outsiders. Conflict between craft and industrial unions has existed for a hundred years. In fact, union "scabs" from the craft-oriented AFL helped break northeastern factory strikes in the early twentieth century.[1] From the 1930s through the 1950s, the AFL's International Brotherhood of Teamsters competed with CIO unions for members and sometimes fought them physically.[2]

Union corruption is not a thing of the past either. Tom Geoghegan, a strong believer in the labor movement at its best, recalled how officers of a Chicago-area Teamsters local beat up a member at his own grievance hearing in the 1980s. Unfortunately, Geoghegan wrote, the Landrum-Griffin Act protections for union democracy had become "something of a joke" in practice.[3] It was not until 1999 that a powerful local SEIU leader, Gus Bevona of New York City, lost his $450,000 salary and marble-paved penthouse above SEIU headquarters.[4]

Not all unions are on working people's side.

Union leaders can become too friendly with management. Geoghegan describes what United Steelworkers dissident Ed Sadlowski faced in the dramatically contested union election of 1976: "The leaders of the Steelworkers were regarded as 'mature,' 'responsible,' 'statesmanlike.' Men like I.W. Abel, the Union president, and Lloyd McBride, his heir apparent, were then the darlings of the editorial pages. Men so 'mature,' so 'responsible,' they had given up the right to strike."[5]

Nelson Lichtenstein writes that anticommunism and the antiunion mood created by the Senate McClellan Committee's corruption hearings frightened unions in the 1950s. One writer at the time said labor had "lost the intellectuals." They gave up on social change and stuck to dull, safe "business unionism."[6] He notes that in the 1960s, liberal economist John Kenneth Galbraith thought unions had lost power by becoming lesser members of an economic bureaucracy alongside business and government, rather than keeping their outsider status.[7]

Snobbery toward poor people is another union fault. SEIU locals at first disdained efforts to unionize "workfare" workers in New York City, San Francisco, and elsewhere. Workfare workers were required to put in assigned hours for city departments to earn their welfare checks and received less pay per hour, under worse conditions, than conventionally employed city workers. It took a while to realize that the new and old unions were on the same side: both wanted city work to be performed by full-time workers at living wages, not by underpaid part-timers deprived of normal employee protections. The San Francisco and New York groups eventually won some respect and concessions from both unions and local governments.[8]

In the 1990s, R.G. Goudy, an early member of the San Francisco workfare union POWER, became ill one day from a strong cleaning chemical he was told to use on graffiti inside a city bus. A regular employee would have gotten an emergency checkup; POWER organizers argued all day to get him the same. Goudy recalls, "While I was doing workfare for [the city bus system], car cleaners had dropped to about 15% of the number [the system employed] before workfare was instituted. The position of 'car cleaner' had been transferred to a pseudomanagement job as they no longer actually cleaned cars."[9]

In another example of union snobbery, an article by SEIU and other organizers acknowledges that at the start of the Justice for Janitors campaign, the union's internal problems included "a tendency to view immigrant workers as the enemy; rather than embracing and organizing immigrants, many in SEIU blamed them for the growth of non-union low-wage contractors."[10]

Unions are also sometimes accused of going beyond healthy persuasion in their "get out the vote" efforts. The ballot is secret, but muscular men offering rides to the polls can make it difficult for voters to say no. While it is normal and legal for campaign representatives to monitor polling places, monitors can sometimes become menacing presences.[11]

During the 2008 presidential election, there were many complaints about union involvement in Barack Obama's campaign. The National Right to Work Committee and its legal arm pursued complaints that an Alabama teachers union diverted money from travel budgets to pro-Obama contributions and that unions were spending "forced dues" on Obama.[12]

Racism and other prejudice are ingrained parts of organized labor.

Unfair job discrimination is not just a bad habit in the labor movement. For many unions it has been a central purpose of their existence. Discrimination may even be inevitable in unions to the extent that it is their purpose to defend insiders against outsiders. At one time, unions allowed only white men to join, presuming that women, members of minority groups, and immigrants would always be easier to push around and therefore would always settle for lower pay. Of course, a worker who lacks

Untrustworthy Trusteeships?

Trusteeship refers to a national union office taking over a local union and appointing a "trustee" to run the union from above. In such an instance, members of a local cannot elect their own local leaders. Trusteeship is intended to clean up local corruption or other misconduct, and sometimes it is used for that purpose, but it can also be used in plain power plays. For example, the McClellan hearings addressed examples of corrupt trusteeships in the International Brotherhood of Teamsters.

A recent trusteeship fight in the SEIU provoked allegations of bullying at United Healthcare Workers–West (UHW-West), a union within the SEIU that represents 150,000 California nursing home and home health-care staffers. The international SEIU, under President Andy Stern, placed UHW-West under trusteeship after a feud with its outspoken leader, Sal Rosselli. Stern's office claimed Rosselli and other UHW-West officers had misused union funds by putting $3 million into a nonprofit group for health-care issue campaigns. As of 2009, Rosselli and his allies were collecting signatures to decertify the SEIU as bargaining representative of workers at a series of hospitals and nursing homes. (A petition signed by 30 percent of a workforce can trigger a decertification election.)

In the fight that led to the trusteeship, Rosselli told the *San Francisco Chronicle*, "This is worse than any 'boss' campaign we have ever been through. . . . It is like a strike." With the two factions trading corruption allegations, the whole mess left outsiders wondering which side to trust, if either.

Sources: George Raine, "Unions Battle Over Health Care Workers," *San Francisco Chronicle*, December 7, 2008, http://www.sfgate.com/cgi-bin/article.cgi?f=/c/a/2008/12/06/BU6K14IPH8.DTL; Raine, "Ousted SEIU Leaders Push Decertification Vote," *San Francisco Chronicle*, February 3, 2009, http://www.sfgate.com/cgi-bin/article.cgi?f=/c/a/2009/02/03/BU1L15LO03.DTL; Raine, "Half of State's Kaiser Workers Want Vote About Dropping SEIU," *San Francisco Chronicle*, February 27, 2009; Paul Pringle, "Scandals Scar Triumphs for Head of SEIU," *Los Angeles Times*, December 31, 2008, http://articles.latimes.com/2008/dec/31/local/me-stern31; Mark Brenner, "Under Shadow of Corruption Scandals, SEIU Launches Hearings Against Dissidents," *Labor Notes*, http://www.labornotes.org/node/1919; United Healthcare Workers–West, "Q&A for SEIU UHW-W Members Regarding the Trusteeship," http://www.seiu-uhww.org/frequently-asked-questions-about-th.html.

union support really is easier to push around, so this approach both created victims and blamed them.

Anti-Asian protectionism was a key part of the West Coast labor movement from the middle of the nineteenth century well into the twentieth century. Notable among the incidents were the bloody anti-Chinese riots of 1877. Shamefully, the "union label"—a label, usually on clothing or printed material, with the emblem of the union that handled it—has its origins in a California anti-Chinese campaign that promoted boots and cigars made with "white labor."[13] Samuel Gompers of the early American Federation of Labor pressed unions to give up antiblack racism but helped campaigns against workers of Chinese descent.[14]

Before employment sexism became illegal, many (not all) union members thought it was a heroic defense of their living standards to keep women out of industrial workplaces. Jack London, writing in 1904, observed that women and children were often caught in circumstances that required them to go against what he saw as the working class's interests: "The woman stenographer or bookkeeper who receives forty dollars per month where a man was receiving seventy-five is a scab. So is the woman who does a man's work at a weaving machine, and the child who goes into the mill or factory. And the father, who is scabbed out of work by the wives and children of other men, sends his own wife and children to scab in order to save himself."[15] He did not suggest paying women fairly.

Sociologist Paul Frymer writes that when the National Labor Relations Act passed in 1935, the NAACP estimated that unions had only 50,000 African-American members, of whom half were in the all-black Brotherhood of Sleeping Car Porters, while many of the rest were in segregated unions with reduced rights. In enforcing the NLRA, the National Labor Relations Board allowed obvious racism to continue by certifying all-white unions. Until the Taft-Hartley Act banned "closed shop" contracts, racist unions could keep workplaces all white through the employer's agreement to hire only people who were already union members.

In *Steele v. Louisville & Nashville R. Co.*, the Supreme Court ruled that unions have a duty of "fair representation" regardless of race.[16] However, that decision only addressed unions' discrimination against already accepted members. The agencies and courts failed to address outright exclusion from membership, which remained a problem. Even in 1963, an investigation by the federal Committee on Equal Employment Opportunity found that nine construction trade unions were still all white.

The Civil Rights Act of 1964 was more lenient toward racism in its labor-related Title VII than in other areas like school integration. The law at first denied the newly created Equal Employment Opportunity Commission (EEOC) strong enforcement powers against private employers, cramped the issues and remedies the EEOC could pursue, and put a heavy burden of proof on people who complained of discrimination. President Lyndon Johnson set the first affirmative-action hiring goals for federal contractors with his Executive Order 11246 in 1969. Soon after, President Richard Nixon tried to integrate construction unions. However, unions had enough political muscle to ignore both without real consequences.

Congress finally gave the EEOC real enforcement power against private employers in the 1970s. Integration of unions began through EEOC actions and private individuals suing unions in the 1970s and early 1980s. Court desegregation orders made unions accept more African-American and other minority members. One union, the Sheet Metal Workers Local 28 in New York City, changed from zero minority membership in 1970 to 20 percent by the end of the 1980s, but it also went bankrupt over a court judgment for back wages owed because of discrimination.[17]

Paul Frymer writes that the integration period did not end unions' role as alleged perpetrators of racism, only that new sorts of charges emerged. From 1935 to 1966, he found that charges of racism in NLRB cases almost uniformly involved southern employers who tried to divide white from black employees, sometimes with racist threats, during antiunion campaigns. From 1967 to 2000, however, Frymer found that "only 25 percent involved accusations that the employer committed the racist act." Some were backhanded charges made by employers who themselves had been accused of racism by organizers, and union organizers themselves also used racist slurs against employers.[18]

Mainstream unions only represent people with jobs.

Unions, being organizations of employed people, do not represent people who have lost jobs, are looking for jobs, are self-employed, work without pay, or cannot work. (Unions do support retirees and people who have intermittent work like professional screenwriters, and the UAW has famously negotiated continuing benefits for certain laid-off workers.) Still, people in those categories qualify for unions' help based on their work records.[19] Some activist labor groups, like the old IWW, have tried to include unemployed or unpaid workers as members, but without huge success.

Unions cannot, or will not, do much for people who work without pay, without an effective right to quit or leave, or in exchange for food, shelter, and other support. Every society contains people like these. Labels for the worst arrangements include slavery, debt peonage, bonded labor, indentured servitude, and sharecropping. Some feminists would add that women who do unpaid work in families are economically cheated. Even today, it can be a radical step to insist that a person's work should be measured in hours and paid for in money. Unions do not usually do that kind of insisting.

Unions' focus on employment locks them into presuming that a job is always a good thing, and that people with jobs are the ones worth defending. For example, they do not help people share the benefits of new technology. When someone invents a machine to do a dull job that someone used to perform all day in a noisy factory, the displaced worker does not get paid to turn on the machine in the morning and go home. Instead of trying to share out the newly created leisure time fairly, a union's idea of defending that worker may be to keep the job the way it was before, as dull, noisy, toxic, and mind-numbing as ever. Unions do help distribute leisure fairly when they become strong enough to change the length of the workweek, but they cannot easily help specific workers benefit from the innovations that replace them.

Some of the most famous union battles have been hopeless defenses against new technology. One was the fight in early nineteenth-century England against knitting machines that made stockings faster than by hand. Displaced workers calling themselves Luddites, after the fictional leader Ned Ludd, smashed machines in early instances of workplace sabotage (intentional damage).[20] More recently, in the 1960s, labor unions tried to keep newspapers from replacing the old mechanical linotypes, which molded hot lead into a fresh "slug" of type for each line of text. Cleaner, more efficient offset printing allowed fewer people to do the same work without exposure to the danger of fumes from melting lead. Unions fought the offset process so furiously that they drove some newspapers out of business. In an earlier generation, the linotype had taken away the jobs of the typesetters who used to place each individual letter of type by hand into a book or newspaper page. As Mark Twain said of an earlier typesetting machine, "It could work like six men and do everything but drink, swear and go out on strike."[21]

A union is not set up to consider if the world needs a product badly enough to justify what it does to the people who make it. The kind of work that made the mid–twentieth century middle class may have been well paid but it was boring and awful. So says Ben Hamper, a third-generation General Motors "shoprat" in Flint, Michigan, and author of the memoir, *Rivethead: Tales from the Assembly Line.* Factory work was the default future for kids from Hamper's high school who could do no better. He worked eight hours a day riveting GM truck bodies despite noise, boredom, and petty supervisors, then drank too much every night to recover. The pay was good but he hated the work, even when he managed to "double up" jobs with a coworker and spend half of each shift asleep or in a bar. Hamper eventually suffered a mental breakdown and gave up assembly lines for good.

The union did not help Hamper avoid soul-destroying work; it campaigned to keep autoworkers like him in the factories. Hamper describes the union as useful in disputes with supervisors but embarrassing in its clueless distance from the shop floor, as when it cooperated with management to display "inspiring" messages such as "Quality is the Backbone of Good Workmanship!" and, worse, "Squeezing Rivets Is Fun!" Hamper wrote, "I had several definitions of fun. Riveting was nowhere on the list."[22]

People with their own power should not be in unions.

Unions may give unfair additional power to unusual people who already hold a monopoly on irreplaceable skills, like ballplayers and movie stars, or to valuable credentialed professionals like doctors, nurses, and teachers. (Some laws do limit the extent to which public employees, especially medical staff, may go on strike.[23])

Ethical reasons should prevent some other kinds of union members from going on strike, especially police officers and prison guards. When people who have public authority to carry weapons and give orders also assert union power as employees, there can be unethical blurring of their roles. For example, the California Correctional Peace Officers Association, which represents California prison guards, has waged political campaigns for more imprisonment, which means more guarding work to do, thus implying that prison guards know best what protection the public needs.[24]

Unions violate individual rights.

Apart from economic reasons, one can oppose labor unions on philosophical grounds. These start from beliefs in individual rights and private property, both of which are honored and protected in the U.S. Constitution. Some believe unions have not succeeded as well in the United States as elsewhere because of American individualist radicalism. This was the philosophy of Henry David Thoreau and Ralph Waldo Emerson, and arguably of the framers of the Constitution. It is not viewed as just a conservative position. Thoreau, for example, is admired on the left for his 1849 essay, "Civil Disobedience."[25] American radicalism glorifies the individual. It praises "producers," including freelance craftspeople, small business owners, and farmers, as opposed to less evidently useful people such as investors. It criticizes big business and big government equally. Some consider socialism, which has succeeded in countries with the strongest labor unions, as un-American in the sense that it is not consistent with these U.S. philosophical traditions.[26]

Libertarianism is an economically conservative but socially open-minded doctrine, sometimes radically so. It advocates individual freedom as an absolute right, and sees economic bargaining as the fairest means to that freedom.[27] It tends to assume that people enter contracts freely. It believes that government's two principal roles should be to enforce contracts and punish crime. Libertarians believe unions unfairly subordinate the individual to the group. A particularly outspoken strain of libertarianism is the "objectivism" of the late author Ayn Rand, who declared outright that selfishness was a virtue. Among Rand's prominent admirers is Alan Greenspan, who served as Federal Reserve chair from 1987 to 2006.[28]

Anarchists also oppose government interference with the individual, but see market- and property-based systems as unfair to the weaker parties involved. The most difficult question for an anarchist is how to stop bullies without becoming one. Anarchists participated in the early labor movement, especially the IWW, as idealists who believed an organization of powerless people could remain egalitarian if it gained power.[29] Anarchism lost influence around the time of World War I through political backlash against versions of the doctrine that called for violence, and with growing evidence that "people's" organizations and governments could harden into oppressive hierarchies.

Who's the Underdog Here?

What connects medieval guild masters, doctors, lawyers, *Buffy the Vampire Slayer*, and a major league infielder to be named later? They are all members of labor organizations.

Unions have a double ancestry in the European countries that colonized the Americas. On one hand, they hail from the grassroots movements that helped invent modern democracy. On the other hand, they descend from the craft guilds of old Europe. The guilds were powerful groups of skilled professionals that existed in part to maintain professional standards but also to keep prices high by limiting membership in their professions. Modern unions were invented by hungry laborers looking up at the power structure, and partly by wealthy men looking down from within it. It is a mismatch of perspectives that has caused identity confusion in the labor movement for centuries.

Not all labor organizations call themselves unions. Legal and medical licensing boards are also labor organizations to the extent that they work with leading members of the professions to decide who may call themselves doctors or lawyers. When members of a state attorney licensing board decide to reduce the crop of new lawyers by making the next bar exam more difficult, they are using a fee-raising technique familiar to the builders of Europe's cathedrals.

The Major League Baseball Players Association (MLBPA) is a popular example in any argument that unions can make the rich richer. The MLBPA's average member salary rose from $14,863 per season in 1964 (that's $101,847.51 in 2008 dollars) to more than $3 million in 2008. Alex "A-Rod" Rodriguez held the record salary as of 2008: $28 million. Baseball ticket prices rose during the same period. (The increases are also sometimes blamed on building new stadiums, which are paid for in part by taxpayer dollars.) From the mid-1960s through the mid-1990s, average ticket prices

Both libertarians and anarchists dislike rigid rules and involuntary memberships. They oppose "statist" responses to inequality such as Social Security benefits, national health services, and progressive income taxation. Unions usually support the "statist" position that government should provide services such as pensions and health care.

ranged between about $11 and about $15 in 2008-equivalent dollars. Then they shot upward. In 2008, the average Major League Baseball ticket price was $25.40.*

How does the cast of *Buffy the Vampire Slayer* get into this story? They are members of the Screen Actors Guild (SAG), an organization that secures residual payments for members when their productions are shown in commercial ventures. Popular fan sing-along events were shut down because of these residual payments.

It started with a party theme: Fans would get together in costume to sing along with the show's movie-musical episode, "Once More With Feeling." In 2007, some fans took the idea on tour. They produced "Buffyoke" midnight movie events in the style of *Rocky Horror Picture Show* sing-alongs. The events were popular, sometimes hundreds attended, but as MTV News reported the organizers "weren't necessarily making a profit."

Midway through the tour, SAG sent "a six-figure bill for unpaid actor residuals" to Fox Television, which owns the musical episode. A dispute developed with Fox about whether the fans had bought sufficient licensing rights for the tour. Fox then canceled the events, leaving thousands of fans dressed up with no place to go. As *Buffy* creator Joss Whedon said, "it's lousy news and it's bad business."**

*Michael J. Haupert, "The Economic History of Major League Baseball." EH.Net Encyclopedia, http://eh.net/encyclopedia/article/haupert.mlb; CBSSports.com, "MLB Salaries," http://www.cbssports.com/mlb/salaries/avgsalaries and http://www.cbssports.com/mlb/salaries/top50; Boston.com, "Major League Baseball Average Ticket Prices," http://www.boston.com/sports/baseball/articles/2008/03/28/average_ticket_price_list/; CPI Inflation Calculator, http://data.bls.gov/cgi-bin/cpicalc.pl.

**Jennifer Vineyard, "Buffy The Vampire Slayer' Sing-Alongs Killed . . . but Can They Be Resurrected?" MTV News, October 15, 2007, http://www.mtv.com/news/articles/1571966/20071015/index.jhtml; "All Upcoming Shows Have Been Canceled Without Notice!" Uncoolkids.com, http://uncoolkids.com/buffy/?page_id=2.

Summary

Not all unions are on working people's side. Unions can abuse their own members, enrich leaders, or get too close to employers. Racism and other forms of prejudice are not just bad habits with unions; they follow from unions' basic purpose to protect in-groups against outsiders. Unions sometimes protect people who already have excessive bargaining power. Unions are also limited by their roles as representatives of people employed in conventional jobs. Philosophical opponents of unions may argue that they unfairly restrain individual rights. Unions may have had less success in the United States than elsewhere because of the American individualist tradition.

What's Ahead

Unions may be reclaiming their old position of honor as defenders of working people in trouble. Unfortunately, that is because workers in the United States are facing very difficult times.

A relatively pro-labor president could mean huge changes ahead. There have been other Democratic presidents in office since labor's decline began, but President Obama owes more than most to unions' support, and as a result he shows unusual sympathy toward unionization. (Accusations of union corruption, especially at the SEIU, resurfaced alongside this new sign of union power.[1]) Major pro-union changes are possible, especially when Obama appointed Hilda Solis as secretary of labor. In particular, the pending EFCA could increase unionization dramatically if passed. There are additional possibilities in the air. For example, as Tom Geoghegan began his candidacy for Congress, he called for adding union membership to characteristics protected by the Civil Rights Act.[2]

Some of Obama's early presidential decisions affecting labor have sparked protests. When he appointed Democratic member Wilma Liebman to chair the National Labor Relations Board, an editorial at the National Right to Work Legal Defense Foundation fumed, "Naked Advocate of Forced Unionism Named NLRB Chair."[3] Then, within days of taking office, Obama issued three executive orders that strengthened unions and employees' rights in federal contracting while they discouraged antiunion campaigns by federal contractors.[4] Another order allowed federal agencies to require the use of uniform "project labor agreements" on some large federal contracts. The Associated Builders and Contractors responded to that one with a press release headed, "ABC Denounces Executive Order That Discriminates Against 84 Percent of the Construction Workforce," meaning that the agreements could require union-only contractors and shut out all others.[5]

In 2009, the future of traditional factory labor unions seemed threatened by losses in the U.S. auto industry, as failing automakers pressed unions to give up jobs and existing contracts. General Motors and Chrysler reorganized through government-engineered bankruptcies and bailouts. Chrysler was purchased by the Italian automaker Fiat and continued a program of layoffs. General Motors became majority-owned by the U.S. government, with other shares going to the Canadian and Ontario provincial governments. The United Auto Workers accepted a 17.5 percent stake in GM, to partly fund a medical benefits trust for retirees in place of earlier contracts' health guarantees. According to the AFL-CIO, the GM bankruptcy judge took away health care coverage from 55,000 retired members of other unions. With the UAW's support, these other union members were campaigning to get their coverage back. Although the new GM was partly union-owned, it was expected to close down whole categories of production, causing huge layoffs.[6]

These demands are arguably examples of what writer Naomi Klein calls "disaster capitalism": the conscious use of economic, natural, or military disasters to extract concessions from poorer countries or people, often by privatizing public resources or services.[7] In another example of "disaster capitalism," Hearst Corp. threatened to close the money-losing

QUOTABLE

President Barack Obama

The first bill President Barack Obama signed was the Lilly Ledbetter Fair Pay Act 2009, now Public Law 111-2, in which Congress responded to the Supreme Court Ledbetter decision by overriding the court's interpretation of fair pay rights. The new law says an employer violates an employee's rights with each act of discrimination, whether or not the employee finds out. It allows victims of discrimination to recover back pay for wage discrimination for periods up to two years before they file a charge. The following are excerpts from President Obama's remarks:

So signing this bill today is to send a clear message: that making our economy work means making sure it works for everybody; that there are no second-class citizens in our workplaces; and that it's not just unfair and illegal, it's bad for business to pay somebody less because of their gender or their age or their race or their ethnicity, religion or disability; and that justice isn't about some abstract legal theory, or footnote in a casebook. It's about how our laws affect the daily lives and the daily realities of people: their ability to make a living and care for their families and achieve their goals.

Ultimately, equal pay isn't just an economic issue for millions of Americans and their families, it's a question of who we are—and whether we're truly living up to our fundamental ideals; whether we'll do our part, as generations before us, to ensure those words put on paper some 200 years ago really mean something—to breathe new life into them with a more enlightened understanding that is appropriate for our time.

Source: "Remarks by the President Upon Signing the Lilly Ledbetter Bill," January 29, 2009 http://www.whitehouse.gov/the_press_office/RemarksbythePresidentUponSigningthe LillyLedbetterBill/.

San Francisco Chronicle newspaper just as it entered negotiations with the paper's staff union. Days later, the union accepted a contract that gave up 150 jobs.[8]

The SEIU and other service unions were making stronger progress than manufacturing unions, but Geoghegan, for one, thought that might not be enough. He wrote recently that "a labor movement based on the service sector can never truly 'come back' as a real force for social democracy . . . in a developed country, no labor movement can succeed if it loses its base in manufacturing."[9]

Summary

The times are frightening but promising for American labor. President Obama sent several strong pro-labor messages during his first days in office. Pro-labor proposals such as the EFCA could become law. However, in the current economic recession, large companies are trying to use their own losses to force concessions from unions. Some observers have argued that unions are past their prime, that they are no longer the kinds of groups working people need to make themselves heard. Others contend unions are exactly what we need to make the United States a fairer and healthier country. The next few years should test both theories.

Beginning Legal Research

The goals of each book in the POINT/COUNTERPOINT series are not only to give the reader a basic introduction to a controversial issue affecting society, but also to encourage the reader to explore the issue more fully. This Appendix is meant to serve as a guide to the reader in researching the current state of the law as well as exploring some of the public policy arguments as to why existing laws should be changed or new laws are needed.

Although some sources of law can be found primarily in law libraries, legal research has become much faster and more accessible with the advent of the Internet. This Appendix discusses some of the best starting points for free access to laws and court decisions, but surfing the Web will uncover endless additional sources of information. Before you can research the law, however, you must have a basic understanding of the American legal system.

The most important source of law in the United States is the Constitution. Originally enacted in 1787, the Constitution outlines the structure of our federal government, as well as setting limits on the types of laws that the federal government and state governments can enact. Through the centuries, a number of amendments have added to or changed the Constitution, most notably the first 10 amendments, which collectively are known as the "Bill of Rights" and which guarantee important civil liberties.

Reading the plain text of the Constitution provides little information. For example, the Constitution prohibits "unreasonable searches and seizures" by the police. To understand concepts in the Constitution, it is necessary to look to the decisions of the U.S. Supreme Court, which has the ultimate authority in interpreting the meaning of the Constitution. For example, the U.S. Supreme Court's 2001 decision in *Kyllo v. United States* held that scanning the outside of a person's house using a heat sensor to determine whether the person is growing marijuana is an unreasonable search—if it is done without first getting a search warrant from a judge. Each state also has its own constitution and a supreme court that is the ultimate authority on its meaning.

Also important are the written laws, or "statutes," passed by the U.S. Congress and the individual state legislatures. As with constitutional provisions, the U.S. Supreme Court and the state supreme courts are the ultimate authorities in interpreting the meaning of federal and state laws, respectively. However, the U.S. Supreme Court might find that a state law violates the U.S. Constitution, and a state supreme court might find that a state law violates either the state or U.S. Constitution.

Not every controversy reaches either the U.S. Supreme Court or the state supreme courts, however. Therefore, the decisions of other courts are also important. Trial courts hear evidence from both sides and make a decision, while appeals courts review the decisions made by trial courts. Sometimes rulings from appeals courts are appealed further to the U.S. Supreme Court or the state supreme courts.

Lawyers and courts refer to statutes and court decisions through a formal system of citations. Use of these citations reveals which court made the decision or which legislature passed the statute, and allows one to quickly locate the statute or court case online or in a law library. For example, the Supreme Court case *Brown v. Board of Education* has the legal citation 347 U.S. 483 (1954). At a law library, this 1954 decision can be found on page 483 of volume 347 of the U.S. Reports, which are the official collection of the Supreme Court's decisions. On the following page, you will find samples of all the major kinds of legal citation.

Finding sources of legal information on the Internet is relatively simple thanks to "portal" sites such as findlaw.com and lexisone.com, which allow the user to access a variety of constitutions, statutes, court opinions, law review articles, news articles, and other useful sources of information. For example, findlaw.com offers access to all Supreme Court decisions since 1893. Other useful sources of information include gpo.gov, which contains a complete copy of the U.S. Code, and thomas.loc.gov, which offers access to bills pending before Congress, as well as recently passed laws. Of course, the Internet changes every second of every day, so it is best to do some independent searching.

Of course, many people still do their research at law libraries, some of which are open to the public. For example, some state governments and universities offer the public access to their law collections. Law librarians can be of great assistance, as even experienced attorneys need help with legal research from time to time.

Common Citation Forms

Source of Law	Sample Citation	Notes
U.S. Supreme Court	*Employment Division v. Smith*, 485 U.S. 660 (1988)	The U.S. Reports is the official record of Supreme Court decisions. There is also an unofficial Supreme Court ("S. Ct.") reporter.
U.S. Court of Appeals	*United States v. Lambert*, 695 F.2d 536 (11th Cir.1983)	Appellate cases appear in the Federal Reporter, designated by "F." The 11th Circuit has jurisdiction in Alabama, Florida, and Georgia.
U.S. District Court	*Carillon Importers, Ltd. v. Frank Pesce Group, Inc.*, 913 F.Supp. 1559 (S.D.Fla.1996)	Federal trial-level decisions are reported in the Federal Supplement ("F. Supp."). Some states have multiple federal districts; this case originated in the Southern District of Florida.
U.S. Code	Thomas Jefferson Commemoration Commission Act, 36 U.S.C., §149 (2002)	Sometimes the popular names of legislation—names with which the public may be familiar—are included with the U.S. Code citation.
State Supreme Court	*Sterling v. Cupp*, 290 Ore. 611, 614, 625 P.2d 123, 126 (1981)	The Oregon Supreme Court decision is reported in both the state's reporter and the Pacific regional reporter.
State Statute	Pennsylvania Abortion Control Act of 1982, 18 Pa. Cons. Stat. 3203-3220 (1990)	States use many different citation formats for their statutes.

Cases

Commonwealth v. Pullis (1806)

The 1806 "Philadelphia Cordwainers Case," in which the Philadelphia mayor's court convicted shoemakers of threatening fellow workers so they would join in a wage demand.

In Re Debs, 158 U.S. 564 (1895)

This decision upheld a federal district court decision, *U.S. v. Debs*, 64 F. 724 (N.D. Ill. 1894), which issued criminal contempt sentences to union organizers who violated an injunction not to slow down U.S. mail during the Pullman Strike.

Lochner v People of State of New York, 198 U.S. 45 (1905)

The U.S. Supreme Court found a worker protection law limiting bakers' wages and hours violated the bakers' own freedom of contract rights.

West Coast Hotel Co. v. Parrish, 300 U.S. 379 (1937); *National Labor Relations Board v. Jones & Laughlin Steel Corp.,* 301 U.S. 1 (1937)

These high court decisions ended the "Lochner era" by approving wage and hour protections and found the National Labor Relations Act to be constitutional.

National Labor Relations Board v. Mackay Radio & Telegraph Co., 304 U.S. 333 (1938)

It was decided that employers may hire "permanent replacement workers" during a strike and keep them afterwards, even at ex-strikers' expense.

U.S. v. Hutcheson, 312 U.S. 219 (1941)

This decision interpreted the Clayton and Norris-LaGuardia Acts to protect a union carpenters' strike against a company that hired a rival union's members for a project.

Youngstown Sheet & Tube Co. Et al. v. Sawyer, 343 U.S. 579 (1952)

This U.S. Supreme Court decision upheld President Harry Truman's decision to order U.S. steelmakers back to work during a labor dispute.

United Steelworkers of America v. American Manufacturing Co., 363 U.S. 564; *United Steelworkers of America v. Warrior & Gulf Navigation Co.,* 363 U.S. 574, and *United Steelworkers of America v. Enterprise Wheel & Car Corp.,* 363 U.S. 593 (all 1960)

Known as the "Steelworker's Trilogy," these three cases together held that once an arbitrator has issued a decision, the only question for a court is whether the arbitrator had power under the contract to issue the decision, not whether the decision was fair.

Boys Markets v. Clerks Union, 398 U.S. 235 (1970)

The U.S. Supreme Court banned strikes over issues "arbitrable" under a union contract.

Gateway Coal Co. v. Mine Workers, 414 U.S. 368 (1974)

The high court held that strikes are illegal even over mine safety disputes if the union contract makes the dispute arbitrable.

NLRB v. Weingarten, Inc., 420 U.S. 251 (1975)

This case established workers' right to have a union shop steward present during interviews that may result in discipline.

Hoffman Plastic Compounds v. Labor Relations Board, 535 U.S. 137 (2002)

In this case, the Supreme Court found that when an undocumented worker is fired for organizing, the usual unfair labor practice remedy of back pay is unavailable because this worker has no right to earn wages in the United States.

Lilly Ledbetter v. Goodyear Tire & Rubber Co., Inc., 550 U.S. 618 (2007)

In this case, the U.S. Supreme Court found that a victim who learned belatedly of 20 years of gender discrimination filed her complaint too late to recover payment. Legislatively overruled by the Lilly Ledbetter Fair Pay Act of 2009.

Davenport v. Washington Education Association, 551 U.S. ____ (2007)

In this case, it was found that unions that collect fees from nonmembers may require their specific permission to use the fees for political spending.

Locke v. Karass, U.S. Supreme Court, 555 U.S. ____ (2009)

The U.S. Supreme Court decided that a union could legally contribute a portion of nonmembers' "service fees" for use by the Service Employees International Union (SEIU) in pro-union litigation.

Ysursa v. Pocatello Education Association, 555 U.S. ____ (2009)

The U.S. Supreme Court found that an Idaho state law did not violate First and Fourteenth amendment rights when it allowed payroll deductions for union dues but prohibited payroll deductions for union political purposes.

Statutes

Clayton Act (1914)

This federal law took early steps against antiunion court injunctions.

Davis-Bacon Act (1931)

A federal law requiring "prevailing wages" on federal contracts, which has been amended many times and supplemented by companion laws.

Norris-La Guardia Act (1932)

A federal law that banned most antiunion court injunctions.

National Labor Relations Act (1935)

This federal law, also known as the Wagner Act, recognized a right to unionize.

Taft-Hartley Act (1947)

The Labor Management Relations Act, a federal law that restricted union tactics, banned the "closed shop," and bureaucratized the union recognition process.

Landrum-Griffin Act (1959)

This federal law further restricted "secondary" tactics that pressured employers through their business contacts. It imposed federal supervision and member disclosure rules designed to fight union corruption.

Civil Rights Act (1964)

This is the principal federal antidiscrimination law of the modern era. The act's Title VII banned racism and sexism in hiring and by unions, and created the Equal Employment Opportunity Commission to enforce employment civil rights.

Age Discrimination in Employment Act (1967)

A federal law that protects older workers.

Occupational Safety and Health Act (1970)

A federal law that created the Occupational Safety and Health Administration.

Rehabilitation Act (1973)

This is an early disability rights law.

The Employee Retirement Income Security Act (1974)

Also known as ERISA, this is a pension protection law.

Americans with Disabilities Act (1990)

A federal law that protects disability rights in many contexts, including employment.

Family and Medical Leave Act (1993)

A federal law that grants limited protections for employees who take time off for illness, childbirth, or family caretaking.

Lilly Ledbetter Fair Pay Act (2009)

A federal law passed in response to the Supreme Court's *Ledbetter* decision. The law provides that rights are violated when discrimination happens, not when the victim learns of the violation. The law allows victims of discrimination to recover back pay for wage discrimination up to two years before a charge is filed.

Terms and Concepts

Arbitration

"Card check" union recognition

Closed shop

Collective bargaining

Company union

Craft union, craft organizing

Employee Free Choice Act (EFCA)

General strike

"Hot cargo" agreement

Industrial union, industrial organizing

Industrial Revolution

Injunction

International union

Local union

Maquiladora
Overtime pay
Permanent replacement workers
Protected concerted activity
Right-to-work laws
Secondary boycott, secondary strike
Sit-down strike
Solidarity
Strike
Sweetheart contract
Sympathy strike
Unfair labor practice
Union
Union authorization card
Union security agreement
Wildcat strike
Yellow-dog contract

Introduction: An Overview of Unions and Labor Laws

1 Thomas Geoghegan, *Which Side Are You On?: Trying to Be for Labor When It's Flat on Its Back*, New York: Plume, 1992, pp. 43-51, 247-250.

2 Karen Ann Cullotta, "Bank Says It Will Consider Loan to Pay Workers in Factory Sit-In," *New York Times*, Dec. 9, 2008, http://www.nytimes.com/2008/12/10/us/10factory.html; Michael Tarm, "Chicago Workers Accept $1.75 Million to End Siege," Associated Press in *San Francisco Chronicle*, Dec. 11, 2008, http://imgs.sfgate.com/cgi-bin/article.cgi?f=/c/a/2008/12/11/BU3114LPVJ.DTL&hw=vacation&sn=158&sc=255.

3 Karen Ann Cullotta, "New Owners to Reopen Window Plant, Site of a Sit-In in Chicago," *New York Times*, February 26, 2009, http://www.nytimes.com/2009/02/27/us/27factory.html.

4 Nelson Lichtenstein and Christopher Phelps, "Chicago Protest Recalls 1936 Sit-In," at "Talking Union: A Project of the DSA Labor Network," Dec. 12, 2008, http://talkingunion.wordpress.com/2008/12/12/chicago-protest-recalls-1936-sit-in/; "The Flint Sit-Down Strike Audio Gallery," Historical Voices, http://www.historicalvoices.org/flint/index.php.

5 U.S. Dept. of Labor, BLS 1980b, table 165, p. 412, tabulated in Michael Goldfield, *The Decline of Organized Labor in the United States*, Chicago: University of Chicago Press, 1987, p. 10; U.S. Dept. Labor, BLS, press release nos. USDL 08-0092 and USDL 09-0095, respectively, http://www.bls.gov/news.release/archives/union2_01252008.pdf and http://www.bls.gov/news.release/archives/union2_01282009.pdf; Peter Whoriskey, "American Union Ranks Grow After 'Bottoming Out,'" *Washington Post*, January 29, 2009, http://www.washingtonpost.com/wp-dyn/content/article/2009/01/28/AR2009012801621.html.

6 *Congressional Record*, February 24, 2009, pp. S2402-S2412.

7 Elaine Chao, official biography, Dept. of Labor, http://www.dol.gov/_sec/abou-tosec/chao.htm; Phillip Babich, "Dirty Business: How Bush and His Coal Industry Cronies Are Covering Up One of the Worst Environmental Disasters in U.S. History," *Salon*, Nov. 13, 2003, http://dir.salon.com/story/tech/feature/2003/11/13/slurry_coverup/index.html.

8 "Tom Geoghegan for Congress," http://www.geogheganforcongress.com/.

9 Joseph G. Rayback, *A History of American Labor*, New York: Macmillan, 1959, pp. 3-7; David R. Roediger, *The Wages of Whiteness: Race and the Making of the American Working Class*, London: Verso, 1991, pp. 23-36; Charles B. Craver, *Can Unions Survive?: The Rejuvenation of the American Labor Movement*, New York: New York University Press, 1993, p. 10.

10 Text at http://www.gutenberg.org/dirs/etext02/wltnt11.txt.

11 *Commonwealth v. Pullis*, quoted in Michael Harper and Samuel Estreicher, *Labor Law: Cases, Materials, and Problems*, 4th ed., Boston: Little Brown, 1996, and sources cited therein.

12 Bruce Laurie, *Artisans Into Workers: Labor in Nineteenth-Century America*, New York: Noonday Press, 1989, pp. 64, 79.

13 English translation at http://www.marxists.org/archive/marx/works/1848/communist-manifesto/.

14 Text at http://www.loc.gov/rr/program/bib/ourdocs/EmanProc.html.

15 U.S. Const., amend. XIII.

16 See J. Anthony Lukas, *Big Trouble: A Murder in a Small Western Town Sets Off a Struggle for the Soul of America*, New York: Simon & Schuster, 1997, pp 175-187; Allan Pinkerton, *The Mollie Maguires and the Detectives*, G.W. Dillingham, 1877 (1887 ed.); Arthur Conan Doyle, *The Valley of Fear*, http://onlinebooks.library.upenn.edu/webbin/gutbook/lookup?num=3289.

17 Previously cited background sources; Alexander Saxton, *The Indispensable Enemy: Labor and the Anti-Chinese Movement in California*, Berkeley: University of California Press, 1971, 1995, pp. 110–116; Nell Irvin Painter, *Standing at Armageddon: The United States,*

1877–1919, New York: W.W. Norton, 1987, 2008, pp. 15–24.

18 James Green, *Death in the Haymarket: A Story of Chicago, the First Labor Movement, and the Bombing That Divided Gilded Age America,* New York: Anchor Books, 2007.

19 Sherman Antitrust Act; July 2, 1890; http://www.ourdocuments.gov/doc.php?flash=false&doc=51.

20 David Nasaw, *Andrew Carnegie,* New York: Penguin, 2006, pp. 390–441.

21 Previously cited background sources and *In Re Debs,* 158 U.S. 564 (1895); Lukas pp. 310–312; see *U.S. v. Hutcheson,* 312 U.S. 219 (1941).

22 198 U.S. 45 (1905).

23 Lukas, passim.

24 Text at http://www.online-literature.com/upton_sinclair/jungle/.

25 "141 Men and Girls Die in Waist Factory Fire," *New York Times,* March 26, 1911, http://www.ilr.cornell.edu/trianglefire/texts/newspaper/nyt_032611_5.html; "The Triangle Factory Fire," Cornell University Library, http://www.ilr.cornell.edu/trianglefire; Craver p. 23.

26 Bruce Watson, *Bread and Roses: Mills, Migrants, and the Struggle for the American Dream,* New York: Viking, 2005.

27 Mark Walker, "An Archaeology of Labor: Research on Ludlow and the 1913–14 Coal War," The Archaeology of the Colorado Coalfield War Project, University of Denver, 1999, http://www.scribd.com/doc/3480341/.

28 38 Stat. 730 (1914).

29 See Archie Green et al., eds., *The Big Red Songbook,* Chicago: Charles H. Kerr, 2007, p. 4.

30 Thomas E. Sheridan, *Arizona: A History,* Tucson: University of Arizona Press, 1995, pp. 181–186.

31 Felix Frankfurter and Nathan Greene, "Congressional Power Over the Labor Injunction," *Columbia Law Review,* vol. 31, no. 3 (Mar. 1931), pp. 385–415; see then-Justice Frankfurter's account in *U.S. v. Hutcheson,* op. cit., and http://www.motherjonesmuseum.org.

32 See the A. Philip Randolph Pullman Porter Museum Web site, http://www.aphiliprandolphmuseum.com; Heidi Benson, "Porters' Road to Success

on 'Rolling Hotels'," *San Francisco Chronicle,* Feb. 11, 2009, http://www.sfgate.com/cgi-bin/article.cgi?f=/c/a/2009/02/11/MNAO15RJQG.DTL; Nelson Lichtenstein, *State of the Union: A Century of American Labor,* Princeton: Princeton University Press, 2002, pp. 196–211.

33 47 Stat. 70 (1932); Geoghegan pp. 40–45.

34 48 Stat. 195 et seq.; formally codified at 15 U.S.C. 703.

35 Thaddeus Russell, *Out of the Jungle: Jimmy Hoffa and the Remaking of the American Working Class,* New York: Knopf, 2001, pp. 34–37.

36 *Schechter Poultry Corp. v. United States,* 295 U.S. 495 (1935); 49 Stat. 449 (1935); Goldfield, p. 10.

Point: Unions Are Good for Society

1 Painter, p. 13; Green, pp. 34–35.

2 52 Stat. 1060 (29 U.S.C. 201 et seq.); Jared Bernstein and Ross Eisenbrey, "Eliminating the Right to Overtime Pay: Department of Labor Proposal Means Lower Pay, Longer Hours for Millions of Workers," Briefing Paper #139, Economic Policy Institute, posted June 26, 2003, http://www.epi.org/publications/entry/briefingpapers_flsa_jun03/; see http://www.dol.gov/esa/whd/flsa/.

3 See Chapter 1 and http://northland-poster.com/blog/2007/01/25/the-folks-who-brought-you-the-weekend/; "A Weekend History Lesson," http://weekendamerica.publicradio.org/display/web/2007/11/24/a_weekend_history_lesson/; Eisenbrey and Bernstein.

4 Frederick L. Hoffman, "Industrial Accidents," *Bulletin of the Bureau of Labor,* September, 1908, no. 78, vol. XVII, U.S. Govt. Printing Office, 1909, p. 418, http://books.google.com/books?id=7tQoAAAAYAAJ.

5 U.S. Dept. of Labor, Bureau of Labor Statistics, news release no. USDL 08-1182, August 20, 2008, http://www.bls.gov/news.release/cfoi.nr0.htm.

6 Nasaw, p. 312.

7 Philip Shenon, "Made in the USA?: Hard Labor on a Pacific Island," *New York Times,* July 18, 1993, http://www.nytimes.com/1993/07/18/world/made-

usa-hard-labor-pacific-island-special-report-saipan-sweatshops-are-no.html. House Committee on Resources, *Oversight Hearing on the Enforcement of Federal Laws and the Use of Federal Funds in the Northern Mariana Islands*, 106th Cong., first session, 1999; Senate Committee on Energy and Natural Resources, *Conditions in the Commonwealth of the Northern Mariana Islands*, 110th Cong., first session, 2007.

8 See Barry Yeoman, "Silence in the Fields," *Mother Jones*, Jan/Feb. 2001, http://www.motherjones.com/news/feature/2001/01/farm.html; House Subcommittee on Workforce Protections, *Child Labor Enforcement: Are We Adequately Protecting Our Children?* 110th Cong., second session, 2008.

9 David R. Roediger, *Working Toward Whiteness: How America's Immigrants Became White: The Strange Journey from Ellis Island to the Suburbs*, New York: Basic Books, 2005.

10 Barbara Ehrenreich, *Nickel and Dimed: On (Not) Getting by in America*, New York: Metropolitan Books, 2001, p. 210.

11 U.S. Census population clock, http://www.census.gov/main/www/popclock.html.

12 USDL 09-0095 (See Chapter 1, n. 5 above.)

13 USDL 09-0095, op. cit.

14 Rick Fantasia and Kim Voss, *Hard Work: Remaking the American Labor Movement*, Berkeley: University of California Press, 2004, p. 29. (*Hard Work* has been used as a background source throughout this book.)

15 Search "Horatio Alger" http://onlinebooks.library.upenn.edu/.

16 BLS, "State Occupational Employment and Wage Estimates," http://www.stats.bls.gov/oes/current/oessrcst.htm; G. Andrew Bernat Jr., "Convergence in State Per Capita Personal Income, 1950–99," *Survey of Current Business*, U.S. Dept. of Commerce, Bureau of Economic Analysis, June 2001, pp. 36–48, http://www.bea.gov/scb/pdf/2001/06june/0601cspi.pdf; Morton J. Marcus, "Average Wage Trends Inside and Outside Indiana," *In Context*, Indiana Business Research Center, May-June

2004, http://www.incontext.indiana.edu/2004/may-jun04/news.html.

17 "Landmark Study Shows Mexican Maquiladora Workers Not Able to Meet Basic Needs on Sweatshop Wages," UAW, At Issue, June 29, 2001, http://www.uaw.org/atissue/01/062901crea.html.

18 See, T. A. Frank, "Confessions of a Sweatshop Inspector," *Washington Monthly*, April 2008, http://www.washingtonmonthly.com/features/2008/0804.frank.html.

19 Edward Wong, "At Least 74 Miners Dead in China Blast," *New York Times*, February 22, 2009, http://www.nytimes.com/2009/02/23/world/asia/23miners.html and see http://www.chinalaborwatch.org.

20 Keith Bradsher, "Investors Seek Asian Options to Costly China," *New York Times*, June 18, 2008; http://www.nytimes.com/2008/06/18/business/worldbusiness/18invest.html.

21 David Weil, "Mighty Monolith or Fractured Federation? Business Opposition and the Enactment of Workplace Legislation," in Annette Bernhardt et al., eds., *The Gloves-Off Economy: Workplace Standards at the Bottom of America's Labor Market*, Champaign, Ill.: Labor and Employment Relations Association, 2008, p. 298, quoting Richard B. Freeman and James L. Medoff, *What Do Unions Do?*, New York: Basic Books, 1984.

22 Amy Sugimori, "State and Local Policy Models Promoting Immigrant Worker Justice," in *The Gloves-Off Economy*, p. 221, quoting Annette Bernhardt and Siobhán McGrath, 2005, "Trends in Wage and Hour Enforcement by the U.S. Department of Labor, 1975-2004," http://www.brennancenter.org/page/-/d/download_file_8423.pdf.

Counterpoint: Unions Harm Society as a Whole

1 U.S. Chamber of Commerce Web site, "Challenging the Unions' Anti-Growth Agenda: Big Labor's Agenda Is Bad for U.S. Workers and the Economy," http://www.uschamber.com/unions.htm

2 Russell, pp. 23, 53, and passim.

3 See original texts in *U.S. Statutes at Large*, 61 Stat. 136 (1947) and 73 Stat. 519 (1959). Taft-Hartley Act text at http://steelseizure.stanford.edu/legislation/publiclaws136162.pdf. Corresponding current provisions at 29 U.S. Code 141, 151, 401, and 411.

4 Smith Act, 54 Stat. 670 (1940) (18 U.S. Code Sec. 2385); Taft-Hartley Act, 61 Stat. 136 (1947), Sec. 9(h).

5 Lichtenstein p. 162.

6 Maeva Marcus, *Truman and the Steel Seizure Case: The Limits of Presidential Power*, New York: Columbia University Press, 1977; *Youngstown Sheet & Tube Co. Et al. v. Sawyer*, 343 U.S. 579 (1952), http://steelseizure.stanford.edu.

7 Victor Navasky, *Naming Names*, Harmondsworth, U.K.: Penguin Books, 1981, pp. 199–222, 239–246; Russell, pp. 176–178.

8 Russell, p. 178; Budd Schulberg, introduction to Walter Sheridan, *The Fall and Rise of Jimmy Hoffa*, New York: Saturday Review Press, 1972.

9 Russell, pp. 178–209.

10 *Ibid.*, pp. 221–32.

11 *Ibid.*, pp. 184–85.

12 Barry T. Hirsch, "Unionization and Economic Performance: Evidence on Productivity, Profits, Investment, and Growth," in Fazil Mihlar, ed., *Unions and Right-to-Work Laws*, Vancouver, B.C.: Fraser Institute, 1997, pp. 35–70, http://www2.gsu.edu/~ecobth/Fraser_Union_Performance.pdf.

13 U.S. Chamber of Commerce, "Responding to Union Rhetoric: The Reality of the American Workplace: A Series of U.S. Chamber of Commerce White Papers," Labor, Immigration & Employee Benefits Division, U.S. Chamber of Commerce, 2008, http://www.uschamber.com/publications/reports/unionrhetoric.htm. See especially, "Is Unionization the Ticket to the Middle Class? The Real Economic Effects of Labor Unions," http://www.uschamber.com/assets/labor/unionrhetoric_econeffects.pdf, and works cited therein.

14 U.S. Chamber of Commerce, 2008, http://www.uschamber.com/assets/labor/unionrhetoric_workers.pdf.

15 See obituary, John Maynard Keynes, *New York Times*, April 22, 1946.

16 See Irving Kristol, "The Neoconservative Persuasion," *Weekly Standard*, August 25, 2003, http://www.weeklystandard.com/Content/Public/Articles/000/000/003/000tzmlw.asp; Ezra Klein, "A Neoliberal Education," *Washington Monthly*, May 2007, http://www.washingtonmonthly.com/features/2007/0705.klein.html; Charles Peters, "A Neoliberal's Manifesto," *Washington Monthly*, May 1983, http://www.washingtonmonthly.com/features/1983/8305_Neoliberalism.pdf.

17 "Is Unionization the Ticket," p. 5.

18 James Turner, "ETech Preview: Inside Factory China, An Interview with Andrew Huang," *O'Reilly Radar*, Feb. 12, 2009, http://radar.oreilly.com/2009/02/etech-preview-inside-factory-c.html.

19 Cato Institute, Center for Trade Policy Studies, "Outsourcing and Offshoring," 2009, http://www.freetrade.org/issues/outandoff.html; Daniel Ikenson, "'Buy American' Debate Is Not Dead Yet," Cato @ Liberty blog, Feb. 5, 2009, http://www.cato-at-liberty.org/2009/02/05/buy-american-debate-is-not-dead-yet/.

20 Marcus, p. 47.

21 UC–Berkeley, Bancroft Library, Regional Oral History Office, History of the Kaiser Permanente Medical Care Program site, http://bancroft.berkeley.edu/ROHO/projects/kaiser/; "Henry J. Kaiser—Think Big," Oakland Museum of California, http://www.museumca.org/exhibit/exhi_kaiser.html.

22 Chapter 2, n.5, op. cit.

23 Occupational Safety and Health Act, Pub. L. 91-596, (1970) (29 U.S.C. 651 et seq.) and see http://www.osha.gov.

Point: Current Labor Laws Favor Employers

1 Mike Hall, "Union Membership Grows in 2008. When People Can Join Unions, They Do," AFL-CIO Now Blog, Jan. 28, 2009, http://blog.aflcio.org/2009/01/28/union-membership-grows-in-2008-when-people-can-join-unions-they-do/.

2 *U.S. v. Hutcheson*, op. cit.; U.S. Code Vol. 29, Section 151.

3 301 U.S. 1 (1937).

4 Original texts at 49 Stat. 449 (1935); 61 Stat. 136 (1947) and 73 Stat. 519 (1959) (29 U.S.C. 141 et seq., 151 et seq., and 401 et seq.).

5 Miller Center of Public Affairs, Multimedia Archive, "On the Veto of the Taft-Hartley Bill (June 20, 1947)," http://millercenter.org/scripps/archive/speeches/detail/3344.

6 61 Stat. 136 (1947) (29 U.S. Code 141 et seq. and 151 et seq.).

7 29 U.S. Code Secs. 158–159; see, e.g., NLRB "Procedures Guide," http://www.nlrb.gov/publications/Procedures_Guide.htm; Gerald Mayer, "Labor Union Recognition Procedures: Use of Secret Ballots and Card Checks" (RL32930) Washington, D.C.: Congressional Research Service, 2007, http://digitalcommons.ilr.cornell.edu/key_workplace/561/.

8 Seth Michaels, "New Ads: Pass Employee Free Choice Act, Make Economy Work for All," AFL-CIO Now Blog, Jan. 14, 2009, http://blog.aflcio.org/2009/01/14/new-ads-pass-employee-free-choice-act-make-economy-work-for-all/; Esther Kaplan, "Can Labor Revive the American Dream?," *The Nation*, Jan. 7, 2009, http://www.thenation.com/doc/20090126/kaplan.

9 Mayer, "Labor Union Recognition Procedures."

10 Kaplan, "Can Labor Revive"; "Bakery Workers' Struggle Shows Why U.S. Labor Law Must Change," *AFL-CIO News*, Dec. 7, 2005, http://www.aflcio.org/joinaunion/voiceatwork/ns12072005.cfm; "CBC Workers Lead Fight for Employee Free Choice Act," Consolidated Biscuit Company Workers for Dignity, Justice, & Respect! (Web site of the Bakery, Confectionery, Tobacco Workers & Grain Millers International Union), http://bctgm.org/linked%20sites/CBC/cbc_history.html.

11 "MyPrivateBallot.com," http://myprivateballot.com/.

12 Kate Bronfenbrenner, "Uneasy Terrain: The Impact of Capital Mobility on Workers, Wages, and Union Organizing," (2000). Ithaca, N.Y. [electronic version], pp. v and 73, http://digitalcommons.ilr.cornell.edu/reports/3/.

13 Ann Zimmerman and Kris Maher, "Wal-Mart Warns of Democratic Win," *Wall Street Journal*, August 1, 2008, http://online.wsj.com/article/SB121755649066303381.html (Note: The author worked briefly on the plaintiffs' side of *Dukes v. Wal-Mart*, a federal class-action lawsuit accusing Wal-Mart of discrimination against female employees.)

14 304 U.S. 333 (1938).

15 *United Steelworkers of America v. American Manufacturing Co.*, 363 U.S. 564; *United Steelworkers of America v. Warrior & Gulf Navigation Co.*, 363 U.S. 574; *United Steelworkers of America v. Enterprise Wheel & Car Corp.*, 363 U.S. 593 (all 1960).

16 Geoghegan, pp. 28–32; *Boys Markets v. Clerks Union*, 398 U.S. 235 (1970); *Gateway Coal Co. v. Mine Workers*, 414 U.S. 368 (1974).

17 Craver, pp. 48–49.

18 535 U.S. 137 (2002).

19 Lance Compa, "Blood, Sweat and Fear: Workers' Rights in U.S. Meat and Poultry Plants," Human Rights Watch report, 2004, Part VIII, http://www.hrw.org/en/node/11869/section/9.

20 Sugimori, p. 223; Cal. Civil Code Sec. 3339.

21 James Parks, "Labor Board Ruling May Bar Millions of Workers from Forming Unions," AFL-CIO Blog, Oct. 3, 2006, http://blog.aflcio.org/2006/10/03/labor-board-ruling-may-bar-millions-of-workers-from-forming-unions/; *Oakwood Healthcare, Inc.*, 348 NLRB 686 (2006); *Croft Metals, Inc.*, 348 NLRB 717 (2006), and *Golden Crest Healthcare Center*, 348 NLRB 727 (2006).

22 *Dana Corporation*, 351 NLRB 434 (2007); Sholnn Freeman "Labor Board Under Attack," *Washington Post*, Dec. 14, 2007, http://www.washingtonpost.com/wp-dyn/content/article/2007/12/13/AR2007121301926.html; House Subcommittee on Health Employment, Labor and Pensions, and Senate Subcommittee on Employment and Workplace, joint hearing, *The National Labor Relations Board: Recent Decisions and*

Their Impact on Workers' Rights, 110th Cong., first session, 2007.

23 Lichtenstein p. 166; and see National Right to Work Legal Defense Foundation Web site, http://www.nrtw.org/b/rtw_faq.htm.

24 American Federation of Teachers, "Connecting Unions and Civil Rights," http://www.aft.org/topics/civil-rights/mlk/connect.htm.

25 *West Coast Hotel Co. v. Parrish*, 300 U.S. 379 (1937); *National Labor Relations Board v. Jones & Laughlin Steel Corp.*, 301 U.S. 1 (1937); Allison Martens, "Parrying with the Courts: Analyzing the *Lochner* Era Through the Eyes of Organized Labor," presented at the conference of the American Political Science Association, Philadelphia, Aug. 31, 2006, http://www.allacademic.com/meta/p153106_index.html.

26 *Alleluia Cushion Co., Inc.*, 221 NLRB 999 (1975); *Meyers Industries, Inc.*, 268 NLRB 493 (1984).

27 Public Law 88-352 (42 U.S.C. 2000e et seq.).

28 Pub. L. 90-202 (29 U.S.C. 621 et seq.).

29 Pub. L. 91-596 (29 U.S.C. 651 et seq.).

30 Pub. L. 93-112 (29 U.S.C. 701 et seq.).

31 Pub. L. 93-406 (29 U.S.C. 1001 et seq.).

32 Pub. L. 101-336 (42 U.S.C. 12101 et seq.)

33 Pub. L. 103-3 (5 U.S.C. 6381 et seq.; 29 U.S.C. 2601 et seq.).

34 Paul Frymer, "Acting When Elected Officials Won't: Federal Courts and Civil Rights Enforcement in U.S. Labor Unions, 1935–1985," *American Political Science Review*, vol. 97, no. 3, pp. 843–58, 2003, http://ssrn.com/abstract=728904.

35 *Lilly Ledbetter v. Goodyear Tire & Rubber Co., Inc.*, 550 U.S. 618 (2007).

36 John W. Wade et al., *Prosser, Wade and Schwartz's Cases and Materials on Torts*, 9th ed., Westbury, N.Y.: Foundation Press, 1994, pp. 1190–1194; Gregory P. Guyton, "A Brief History of Workers' Compensation," *Iowa Orthopaedic Journal*, vol. 19 (1999): pp. 106–10, http://www.pubmedcentral.nih.gov/articlerender.fcgi?artid=1888620; Lawrence M. Friedman and Jack Ladinsky, "Social Change and the Law of Industrial Acci-

dents," *Columbia Law Review* 67 (1967): pp. 50–82; John Fabian Witt, "The Transformation of Work and the Law of Workplace Accidents, 1842–1910," *Yale Law Journal*, vol. 107 (1998): pp. 1467–1502.

37 Tom Geoghegan, "Infinite Debt: How Unlimited Interest Rates Destroyed the Economy," *Harper's*, April 2009, p. 34.

38 Dept. of Labor Fair Labor Standards Act (FLSA) Web page, http://www.dol.gov/esa/whd/flsa/; "Federal Minimum Wage Rates, 1955–2009," http://www.infoplease.com/ipa/A0774473.html.

39 Zatz, Weil in Bernhardt et al., *Gloves-Off Economy*.

40 See Frances Fox Piven and Richard A. Cloward, *Regulating the Poor: The Functions of Public Welfare*, New York: Pantheon Books, 1971.

41 "Temporary Agricultural Employment of H-2A Aliens in the United States; Modernizing the Labor Certification Process and Enforcement; Final Rule," 73 FR 77110 et seq., Dec. 18, 2008, http://edocket.access.gpo.gov/2008/pdf/E8-29309.pdf.

42 See, e.g., Barry Yeoman, "Silence in the Fields," *Mother Jones*, January/February 2001, http://www.motherjones.com/news/feature/2001/01/farm.html; Lee Romney, "In the Fields, a Rude Awakening," *Los Angeles Times*, Nov. 6, 2006; author's personal communications with guestworkers in Tulelake, Calif., 2006.

Counterpoint: Current Labor Laws Are Unfair to Employers

1 Russell, pp. 135–37.

2 73 Stat. 519 (1959), now 29 U.S. Code 401 et seq.

3 Matthiesen, pp. 152, 342–43.

4 *NLRB v. Weingarten, Inc.*, 420 U.S. 251 (1975).

5 See Randel Johnson et al., "The Union Representation Process under the National Labor Relations Act: Maintaining Employee Free Choice for Over 70 Years," Labor, Immigration & Employee Benefits Division, U.S. Chamber of Commerce, 2008, http://www.uschamber.com/assets/labor/unionrhetoric_nlra.pdf; Center for Union Facts; "When Voting Isn't

Private: The Union Campaign Against Secret Ballot Elections," http://www.unionfacts.com/downloads/report.cardCheck.pdf.

6 Handbill template, Associated Builders and Contractors, http://www.abc.org/files/Government_Affairs/Card_Check/PAYSTUB5.pdf.

7 *Clear Pine Mouldings*, 268 NLRB 1044 (1984).

8 *Consolidated Bus Transit, Inc.*, 350 NLRB 1064 (2007).

9 *Dana Corporation*, op. cit.

10 *Ibid.*; Stefan Gleason, "Am-Bushed by Big Labor," National Review Online, September 3, 2007, http://article.nationalreview.com?q=YzQ3YTIxZTM3MjYxYTEyYzY5MjBmNzNiNTY3YTBhZmE=.

11 Gleason; NLRB, "Board Members Since 1935," http://www.nlrb.gov/about_us/overview/board/board_members_since_1935.aspx; Don McIntosh, "Unions Join Nationwide Protest Against Anti-Union NLRB," *Oregon Labor Press*, Dec. 7, 2007, http://www.nwlaborpress.org/2007/12-7-07NLRB.html; Presidential Nominations PN1256-110 and PN1257-110, received by the 110th Congress on January 25, 2008.

12 *The National Labor Relations Board: Recent Decisions and Their Impact on Workers' Rights*, pp. 5, 16–17.

13 *Locke v. Karass*, U.S. Supreme Court, 555U.S. ____ (2009); "Supreme Court Case May Provide More Employee Protections Against Forced Union Dues," National Right to Work Legal Defense Foundation, press release Oct. 3, 2008, http://www.nrtw.org/press/2008/10/supreme-court-case-may-provide-more-; *Davenport*, 551 U.S. ____ (2007).

14 *Ysursav v. Pocatello Education Association*, 555 U.S. ____ (2009).

15 See HR 697, introduced Jan. 24, 2007, http://thomas.loc.gov/cgi-bin/query/z?c110:H.R.697:.

16 See "NFIB Talking Points: Paid Sick Leave," National Federation of Independent Business, http://www.nfib.com/object/IO_33129.html.

17 Pub. L. 103-3, Feb. 5, 1993, 107 Stat. 6 (5 U.S.C. 6381 et seq.; 29 U.S.C. 2601 et seq.).

18 Pub. L. No. 101-336, 104 Stat. 327 (1990). Now 42 U.S. Code Sec. 12101 et seq.; Example 41, "The Americans With Disabilities Act: Applying Performance and Conduct Standards to Employees with Disabilities," U.S. Equal Opportunity Commission, http://www.eeoc.gov/facts/performance-conduct.html.

19 See Paul Frymer, *Black and Blue: African Americans, the Labor Movement, and the Decline of the Democratic Party*, Princeton, N.J.: Princeton University Press, 2008.

20 "Facts on Executive Order 11246 — Affirmative Action," revised Jan. 4, 2002, Office of Federal Contract Compliance Programs, http://www.dol.gov/esa/ofccp/regs/compliance/aa.htm.

21 Frymer, "Acting When Elected Officials Won't."

22 Harry J. Holzer and David Neumark, "Affirmative Action: What Do We Know?" Urban Institute, Jan. 5, 2006, http://www.urban.org/Uploaded-PDF/1000862_affirmative_action.pdf.

23 See the Department of Labor's "Davis-Bacon and Related Acts" page at http://www.dol.gov/esa/whd/programs/dbra. Davis-Bacon Act, 40 USC 3141 et seq.

24 James Sherk, "Davis-Bacon Wage Provisions Depress the Economy," Jan. 28 and Feb. 5, 2009, Heritage Institute WebMemo 2253, http://www.heritage.org/Research/Labor/wm2253.cfm.

25 "Worker Protection: OSHA Inspections at Establishments Experiencing Labor Unrest," Report No. GAO/HEHS-00-144, General Accounting Office, 2000; http://www.gao.gov/archive/2000/he00144.pdf.

26 Saxton; Roediger, *Working Toward Whiteness*.

Point: Unions Give Working People a Fairer Deal

1 Freeman and Medoff, pp. 3–17.

2 Jack London, "The Scab," *The Atlantic*, January 1904, http://www.theatlantic.com/doc/190401/london-scab.

3 "The Scab," attributed to Jack London; http://cwalocal4250.org/outsourcing/binarydata/The%20Scab.pdf.

4 "Eugene V. Debs" (obituary), *Time*, Nov. 1, 1926.

5 Maud Russell, *Men Along the Shore*, New York: Brussel & Brussel, 1966, pp. 94–95.

6 "The ILWU Story," ILWU Web site, http://www.ilwu.org/history/ilwu-story/ilwu-story.cfm; David F. Selvin, *A Terrible Anger: The 1934 Waterfront and General Strikes in San Francisco*, Detroit: Wayne State University Press, 1996, pp. 34–50.

7 A. H. Raskin, "Pier Union Moves to End Shape-Up and to Adopt Democratic Practices," *New York Times*, June 3, 1953, p. 1; Raskin, "Bridges Reported Seeking Hold Here," *New York Times*, Sept. 11, 1953, p. 29; see, e.g., *NLRB v. Jarka Corp. of Philadelphia*, 198 F.2d 618 (3d Cir., 1952); Andrew Herod, "The Impact of Containerization on Work on the New York–New Jersey Waterfront," *Social Science Docket*, New York and New Jersey State Councils for the Social Studies, vol. 4, no. 1, Winter-Spring, 2004, http://people.hofstra.edu/alan_j_singer/Docket/4%201%20%20Workers.pdf; "The Payoff Port," *Time*, Dec. 15, 1952.

8 Howard Kimeldorf, *Reds or Rackets?: The Making of Radical and Conservative Unions on the Waterfront*, Berkeley: University of California Press, 1988, p. 15.

9 See Anthony DePalma, "On the Waterfront, a Scared Silence," *New York Times*, February 17, 1990, http://www.nytimes.com/1990/02/17/nyregion/on-the-waterfront-a-scared-silence.html; Chris Carlsson, "The Progress Club: 1934 and Class Memory," pp. 67–88, in James Brook et al, eds., *Reclaiming San Francisco: History, Politics, Culture*, San Francisco: City Lights Books, 1998.

10 Matthiesen, pp. 4–5, 121–34, 176.

11 Vanessa Tait, *Poor Workers' Unions: Rebuilding Labor from Below*, Cambridge, Mass.: South End Press, 2005, pp. 79–82, 101–27.

12 Tait, pp. 188–90.

13 Christopher L. Erickson et al., "California's Revolt at the Bottom of the Wage Scale: Justice for Janitors in Los Angeles," *California Policy Options*, 2002, pp. 111 ff., http://www.spa.ucla.edu/calpolicy02/EricksonEtc.pdf; *West Bay Build-ing Maintenance Company*, 312 NLRB 715 (1993).

14 Stephen Lerner, Jill Hurst, and Glenn Adler, "Fighting and Winning in the Outsourced Economy: Justice for Janitors at the University of Miami," *Gloves-Off Economy*, pp. 243–67.

15 Homer Bigart, "War Foes Here Attacked by Construction Workers," *New York Times*, May 9, 1970, http://chnm.gmu.edu/hardhats/warfoes.html.

16 United Students Against Sweatshops, http://www.studentsagainstsweatshops.org; Katrina vanden Heuvel, "Sweet Victory: Coalition for Immokalee Workers Wins," *The Nation*, May 23, 2008, http://www.thenation.com/blogs/edcut/323036.

17 Marc Cooper, "Teamsters and Turtles: They're Together at Last," *Los Angeles Times*, Dec. 2, 1999, p. B011.

18 Nik Theodore et al., "Day Labor and Workplace Abuses in the Residential Construction Industry: Conditions in the Washington, D.C., Region," pp. 91–109, in *Gloves-Off Economy*.

19 U.S. Dept. of Housing and Urban Development, Notice No. PDR-2008-01, Feb. 13, 2008, http://www.huduser.org/datasets/il/il08/Medians_2008.pdf.

20 *The Communist Manifesto*, translation at http://www.marxists.org/archive/marx/works/1848/communist-manifesto/ch01.htm.

21 See AFSCME Web site, "AFSCME–Dr. King and the 1968 AFSCME Memphis Sanitation Strike," http://www.afscme.org/about/1029.cfm.

22 See the A. Philip Randolph Pullman Porter Museum Web site, at www.aphiliprandolphmuseum.com, and Benson, "Porters' Road to Success"; Lichtenstein, pp. 196–211.

23 Lichtenstein, p. 18.

24 Tait, pp. 25–46.

25 *Ibid.*, pp. 129–139.

26 Painter, pp. 182–83 and sources cited therein.

27 See Saxton; Carey McWilliams, *Factories in the Field: The Story of Migratory Farm Labor in California*, Berkeley: University of California Press, 1999; *Personal Justice Denied: Report of the Commission on Wartime Relocation and Internment of*

Civilians, reprinted, Washington, D.C.: Civil Liberties Public Education Fund, 1997, pp. 42–46, 69.

Counterpoint: Unions Help Some Working People at Others' Expense

1 Watson, pp. 137–38, 183.
2 Russell, passim.
3 Geoghegan, pp. 154–56, 178–79, 198.
4 Fantasia and Voss, p. 93.
5 Geoghegan, p. 61.
6 Lichtenstein, pp. 166–71.
7 John Kenneth Galbraith, *The New Industrial State*, London: H. Hamilton, 1967, pp. 262–81; Lichtenstein pp. 167–68, 240.
8 Tait pp. 160–84; author's experience as a San Francisco welfare rights advocate.
9 R.G. Goudy, e-mail message to author, Feb. 24, 2009.
10 Lerner et al., p. 248.
11 Author's experience as election irregularities volunteer.
12 *Waites v. Baldwin County Education Association*, complaint to the U.S. Federal Election Commission, http://www.nrtw.org/files/nrtw/FEC%20NEA%20complaint.pdf; National Right to Work newsletter, vol. 54, no. 9, September 2008, http://www.nrtwc.org/nl/nl200809p1.pdf; compare *Locke v. Karass*.
13 Ira B. Cross, *A History of the Labor Movement in California*, Berkeley: University of California Press, 1935, pp. 136–38; Saxton, p. 74.
14 Frymer, *Black and Blue*, p. 50.
15 London, "The Scab," *The Atlantic*.
16 323 U.S. 192 (1944).
17 Frymer, "Acting When Elected Officials Won't"; Edmund F. Wehrle, "The Vietnam War and Labor's Dalliance with the Nixon White House," *Labor: Studies in Working-Class History of the Americas*, vol. 5, no. 3, Fall 2008, p. 50.
18 Paul Frymer, "Racism Revised: Courts, Labor Law, and the Institutional Construction of Racial Animus," *American Political Science Review*, August 2005, abstracted at http://ssrn.com/abstract=728903.
19 GM Benefits and Services Center FAQ, http://www.layoffbenefits.com/gm/faq/faq.htm; "How to Become a Member,"

Writers Guild of America West, http://www.wga.org/uploadedFiles/who_we_are/fyimember.pdf.
20 E. P. Thompson, *The Making of the English Working Class*, New York: Pantheon Books, 1964.
21 Andrew Zimbalist, "Worker Control over Technology," *The Nation*, November 17, 1979, p. 488.
22 Ben Hamper, *Rivethead: Tales from the Assembly Line*, New York: Warner Books, 1992, pp. 160–61 and passim.
23 See New York State's Taylor Law as explained by the Governor's Office of Employee Relations, http://www.goer.state.ny.us/CNA/bucenter/taylor.html.
24 See materials at the UC–Berkeley Institute for Governmental Studies site, "California Correctional Peace Officers Association," http://igs.berkeley.edu/library/htCaliforniaPrisonUnion.htm.
25 Text at http://eserver.org/thoreau/civil.html.
26 Laurie, pp. 152–53 and passim.
27 See http://www.libertarianism.org/.
28 Ayn Rand Institute, http://www.aynrand.org. See Ayn Rand, "Collectivized 'Rights'," http://www.aynrand.org/site/PageServer?pagename=ari_ayn_rand_collectivized_rights; Harriet Rubin, "Ayn Rand's Literature of Capitalism," *New York Times*, September 15, 2007, at http://www.nytimes.com/2007/09/15/business/15atlas.html.
29 Green, p. 129.

Conclusion: What's Ahead

1 See Steven Greenhouse, "Union is Caught Up in Illinois Bribe Case," *New York Times*, Dec. 11, 2008, http://www.nytimes.com/2008/12/12/us/politics/12union.html; Leslie Wayne, "Labor Group Starts Ad Campaign in Battleground States," *New York Times* The Caucus Web site, September 14, 2008, http://thecaucus.blogs.nytimes.com/2008/09/14/labor-group-starts-ad-campaign-in-battleground-states.
2 David Sirota, "Six Little Words," *San Francisco Chronicle*, July 25, 2008; http://www.sfgate.com/cgi-bin/article.cgi?f=/c/a/2008/07/24/EDPS11UVP9.DTL.
3 Nick Cote, "Naked Advocate of Forced Unionism Named NLRB Chair,"

Freedom@Work, January 23, 2009, http://www.nrtw.org/en/blog/forced-unionism-advocate-named-nlrb-chair01232209.

4 Executive orders 13494 through 13496, in "Presidential Documents," *Federal Register*, February 4, 2009, http://www.access.gpo.gov/su_docs/fedreg/a090204c.html; David Stout, "Obama Moves to Reverse Bush's Labor Policies," *New York Times*, Jan. 31, 2009, http://www.nytimes.com/2009/01/31/business/economy/31obamacnd.html.

5 "ABC Denounces Executive Order That Discriminates Against 84 Percent of the Construction Workforce," Associated Builders and Contractors Web site, Feb. 11, 2009, http://www.abc.org/Newsroom2/News_Letters/2009_Archives/Issue_6/ABC_Denounces_Executive_Order_That_Discriminates_Against_84_Percent_of_the_Construction_Workforce.aspx, dated Feb. 11, 2009; Executive Order 13502, *Federal Register*, February 11, 2009, http://www.access.gpo.gov/su_docs/fedreg/a090211c.html.

6 Tom Walsh, "Obama Could Boast Over Auto Bailout," *Detroit Free Press*, July 12, 2009, http://www.freep.com/article/20090712/COL06/907120567/1210/BUSINESS/Obama-could-boast-over-auto-bailout; Greg Gardner, "Chrysler cuts workforce by 8.7% in '09," *Detroit*

Free Press, July 18, 2009, http://www.freep.com/article/20090718/BUSINESS01/907180310/Chrysler-cuts-workforce-by-8.7--in--09; Joann Muller, "GM: 'We're Not Going Back'," July 10, 2009, *Forbes*, http://www.forbes.com/2009/07/10/general-motors-bankruptcy-business-autos-gm.html; James Parks, "Retirees Were Promised Health Care–GM Deal Breaks the Promise," AFL-CIO Now Blog, http://blog.aflcio.org/2009/07/17/retirees-were-promised-health-caregm-deal-breaks-the-promise/; "GM Retirees Who Lost Health Care Benefits in Bankruptcy Fight to Get Them Back," *Workforce Management*, July 14, 2009, http://www.workforce.com/section/00/article/26/54/50.php.

7 Naomi Klein, "Disaster Capitalists Reap Profits," *The Nation*, July 1, 2008, http://www.thenation.com/doc/20080721/lookout.

8 Sarah Phelan, "The Chronicle Death Watch," *San Francisco Bay Guardian*, March 4, 2009, http://www.sfbg.com/entry.php?entry_id=8162; "Chronicle Workers Vote 10 to 1 for Concessions," *San Francisco Chronicle*, March 15, 2009, http://www.sfgate.com/cgi-bin/article.cgi?f=/c/a/2009/03/14/BA0L16FGNH.DTL&tsp=1.

9 Geoghegan, "Infinite Debt," p. 37.

RESOURCES ||||▷

Books

Doyle, Arthur Conan. *The Valley of Fear.* New York: George H. Doran, 1914.

Laurie, Bruce. *Artisans Into Workers: Labor in Nineteenth-Century America.* New York: Hill & Wang, 1989.

Marx, Karl and Friedrich Engels. *The Communist Manifesto.* Authorized English translation: ed. and annotated by Friedrich Engels. Chicago: C.H. Kerr & Co., 1902.

Sinclair, Upton. *The Jungle.* New York: Doubleday, Page & Co., 1906.

Smith, Adam. *An Inquiry into the Nature and Causes of the Wealth of Nations.* London: W. Strahan and T. Cadell, 1776.

Thoreau, Henry David. *Civil Disobedience.* Westwood, N.J.: F. H. Revell Co., 1964.

Reports

Hoffman, Frederick L. "Industrial Accidents," *Bulletin of the Bureau of Labor,* September 1908, no. 78, vol. XVII, U.S. Govt. Printing Office, 1909.

Oliver, Thomas, ed. *Dangerous Trades: The Historical, Social, and Legal Aspects of Industrial Occupations as Affecting Health.* London: J. Murray, 1902.

Web Sites

Associated Builders and Contractors of Central Florida Employee Free Choice Act Resources
http://www.abccentralflorida.com/efca_resources.htm
This site provides anti-EFCA and general antiunion links.

Holt Labor Library
http://www.holtlaborlibrary.org
The Holt Labor Library's site provides labor history materials.

Mother Jones Museum
http://www.motherjonesmuseum.org
This site provides information about the famous labor leader Mary Harris ("Mother") Jones and links to many labor history sites.

National Labor Relations Board (NLRB)
http://www.nlrb.gov
This independent federal agency's site provides information on all NLRB and ALJ (administrative law judge) decisions since 1935.

Political Advocacy Groups: A Directory of United States Lobbyists

http://www.vancouver.wsu.edu/fac/kfountain/business.html

> The site provides links to many employer-side and some union-side lobbyists on labor issues. It is maintained by Washington State University at Vancouver.

U.S. General Accountability Office (GAO)

http://www.gao.gov

> Formerly the General Accounting Office, this government agency's Web site provides investigative reports by Congress's own auditing team.

U.S. Government Printing Office (GPO)

http://www.gpoaccess.gov

> The U.S. Government Printing Office site includes the Federal Register, Code of Federal Regulations, and congressional hearings and reports. Search for congressional hearing transcripts via http://www.gpoaccess.gov/chearings/search.html.

PICTURE CREDITS

MARTHA BRIDEGAM, J.D., is a lawyer and writer in San Francisco. She holds a B.A. in social studies from Harvard University and a law degree from the University of California's Hastings College of the Law. She has served as an attorney in the areas of poverty law, public benefits law, housing rights, employment discrimination, and estate planning. She has written two previous Chelsea House titles.

ALAN MARZILLI, M.A., J.D., lives in Birmingham, Ala., and is a program associate with Advocates for Human Potential, Inc., a research and consulting firm based in Sudbury, Mass., and Albany, N.Y. He primarily works on developing training and educational materials for agencies of the federal government on topics such as housing, mental health policy, employment, and transportation. He has spoken on mental health issues in 30 states, the District of Columbia, and Puerto Rico; his work has included training mental health administrators, nonprofit management and staff, and people with mental illnesses and their families on a wide variety of topics, including effective advocacy, community-based mental health services, and housing. He has written several handbooks and training curricula that are used nationally and as far away as the territory of Guam. He managed statewide and national mental health advocacy programs and worked for several public interest lobbying organizations while studying law at Georgetown University. He has written more than a dozen books, including numerous titles in the POINT/COUNTERPOINT series.